# RAISED
# BY
# MUSICAL
# MAVERICKS

Copyright © 2019-2020 by Mitch Greenhill/Hillgreen

ISBN: 978-0-578-64445-5

# RAISED BY MUSICAL MAVERICKS

*Recalling life lessons from Pete Seeger, Lightnin' Hopkins, Doc Watson, Reverend Gary Davis and others*

BY MITCH GREENHILL

# CONTENTS

| | |
|---|---|
| *Foreword:* Running with the Herd | 1 |
| 5 Years Old: I Hear a Song | 4 |
| 13 Years Old: Ice Skating with Pete Seeger | 11 |
| A Surrogate Uncle, and What the Well-Dressed Musician Will Wear | 19 |
| 14 Years Old: Theory and Practice with Rolf Cahn | 26 |
| 4 Huntoon Street, Dorchester Lower Mills: A Parade of Musical Visitors | 36 |
| 14 Years Old: Saturday Night and Sunday Morning with Reverend Gary Davis | 53 |
| 15 Years Old: The Artist's Life with Eric von Schmidt | 61 |
| 15 Years Old: Divided Loyalties with Merle Travis | 72 |
| 16 Years Old: Breaking Boundaries with Lightnin' Hopkins | 76 |
| 16-20 Years Old: A Wider World with Jackie Washington | 87 |
| The Big City: New York | 97 |
| The Big Country: Inside of the Outside | 105 |
| The Big World: Larger Struggles | 111 |
| 17-22 Years Old: Geoff Muldaur's School of Hip, and the Cambridge-Boston Music Scene | 117 |

| | |
|---|---|
| 20 Years Old: Recording with Sam Charters | 137 |
| Wanderlust: Target Practice with Hunter Thompson | 141 |
| 23 Years Old: On to California | 150 |
| The View from Doc Watson's Funeral | 155 |
| The View from Mike Seeger's Memorial | 162 |
| Afterword | 169 |
| Acknowledgements | 184 |
| Photo credits and playlist | 187 |

*A musical tribe.* Run Doe Run *by Tej Greenhill*

# FOREWORD
*Running with the Herd*

When I was in my late twenties – between jobs, between marriages, even, as I see now, between stages of my life – I took a gig playing lead guitar in a country-western band in Marshall, California. At such a juncture, the modest roadhouse overlooking Tomales Bay provided a comfortable resting place, despite a grumpy bandleader and his uninspiring choice of tunes.

One of the job's few advantages was its beautiful setting, and another was the soothing hour-long commute along a softly wooded coastline. On one such drive home, after work and after midnight, my guitar and amplifier resting in the bed of my Dodge van, a full moon glowed so brightly and the road was so deserted that I dared to turn off my headlights and let nature illuminate Route 1. As soon as I did, a herd of deer ambled out from the forest. About a dozen of these gentle creatures – mostly yearlings with the stubble of new antlers – glided beside my vehicle, and in front and behind. I felt adopted as a temporary member of their tribe. No longer spooked by my headlights, they ran alongside my van for some time, navigating the coast's circuitous inlets, the click of their hooves on the roadway providing a percussive accompaniment to the drone of my six-cylinder engine. The intense moonlight reflected through the scrub oaks and off my companions, casting their shadows onto the pavement. Eventually we reached what must have been their turf's northern frontier, and they loped away, handing me off to the next stage of my journey.

As I look back, that special sense of inclusion – and its loss – have been a central metaphor in my life. Traveling "with the band" or outside its enchanted contours has been a consistent personal barometer. My early memories of this date back to my thirteenth year, when an informal tribe of musicians started visiting our family and sleeping in the spare bedroom. They too surrounded and embraced me within their magic circle.

On the one hand, I was a normal teenager, dealing with high school and hormones. But at the same time, because my father embarked on a midlife career change into the music business, I was receiving a crash course in the roots of American vernacular music. My dad Manny Greenhill had professional relationships with the musicians described in these pages, and other listeners became their fans and followers. Meanwhile, I was sharing a bathroom with them, having breakfast with them, learning guitar licks from them, and riding home with them, after the concerts and parties.

If I had been more aware at the time, I might have paid closer attention and picked up on things that I'm sure I missed. I might not, for example, have lost that song that Willie Dixon gave me, or missed that party with Mississippi John Hurt. But it was always clear to me, from the first time that Pete Seeger and Sonny Terry stepped into our living room, that these artists would be important to me, though I did not yet comprehend how. It was this tribe of musicians who gave welcoming and sometimes challenging support to this curious kid. As on that moonlit night with the deer, they opened my heart and showed me a way forward.

*In the early 70s, betwixt and between*

## 5 YEARS OLD

*I Hear a Song*

New York, 1949. I'm a five-year-old boy squeezing my mother's hand. We emerge from the subway to a cacophony of horns, engines, and loud voices. I become suddenly aware of large cars barreling towards us from several directions, including just beyond my peripheral vision.

"Hold tight," my mother Leona tells me, and I squeeze harder. "We must stay together," she cautions. Frightened, I press closer, trying to lose myself in the folds of her long skirt. Our destination is not far, or so she tells me. We are on our way to a concert, my first. Stride by stride, we navigate the chaotic streets of Manhattan, a faster world than Brooklyn, where we live. When we arrive, she tells me, a special treat awaits.

The hall is large. Carpeted and lit with delicate fixtures, it provides a welcome shelter from the confusing world outside. I exhale and feel my pulse slowing towards its normal rhythm. We find our seats, high in the balcony, and I turn my focus to the stage. A spotlight circle glows in its center. After a while, a large man steps into it, cups his hand around his ear, and begins to sing.

This, she tells me, is the mighty Paul Robeson, performing a special concert for children. His deep, immense voice renders songs like "Shortnin' Bread," "Deep River," and "Little David Play On Your Harp."

*Little David, play on your harp, hallelu, hallelu*
*Little David, play on your harp, hallelu*

*Paul Robeson*

As we look down on him, Robeson seems like a distant star. A powerful gravitational field seems to emanate from him. I feel myself, as well as those around me – other children and their parents – drawn into its orbit. Within a few songs, we have become a community, bound together by music and by the artist's aura. It's a kind of alchemy, a transporting magic that has changed me. The outside world's dissonance keeps its distance from this harbor of safe harmony.

I want to explore that world. I want to get inside that music.

Back in Brooklyn, fireflies have suddenly appeared in the vacant lot across East 21st Street. They too evoke distant stars, but are nearer, perhaps easier to grasp. In the deepening twilight, I run after the spiraling wisps of light. I want to catch some magic, hold it in my hands. I run after them, but, one after another, the fireflies elude me, dancing and flying just out of my reach. But I see that other kids have caught some of them, and I am determined to get one, too. I redouble my efforts, running faster and jumping higher. When I finally succeed, I'm breathless as the creature glows in my cupped hands. I triumphantly carry it home to our third-floor apartment, and secure it in a jar, the lid screwed tight to prevent escape. I check throughout the evening hours only to discover that, before long, the light fades to a dull ember, then disappears.

The other fireflies, the ones that flew away, have soared off to new adventures. Paul Robeson too has moved on. I experience wanderlust envy, and so with daylight I climb into our DeSoto and attempt the first of my forays into the wider world. This car has a starter pedal on the floor, to the left of the brake and clutch. With the key engaged, the pedal will start the engine, awaken the beast. But I have no key. Still, I press on that starter pedal, over and over again. To reach it, I have to stand, my chest to the steering wheel. The engine responds, groaning, grinding, searching for the spark of life. With each groan, the car lurches a few more inches forward. Exhilarated, I turn the wheel towards the road and the world beyond.

*Mitch, Manny, first guitar lesson*

After a while, I have managed to get the car slanting awkwardly into East 21st Street. But when I turn my head, I see my dad glaring at me through the window. I am discovered, ashamed, busted. Did one of my playmates panic and alert my parents? My father angrily marches me home, after first restoring the car safely to its parking spot. My yearning is shelved for another day.

For now, the open road is Sunrise Highway, the route we take to visit relatives who have already transformed from Brooklyn apartment residents to Long Island suburbanites, with lawns. On the way back, I stretch out and fall asleep on the ledge above the back seat. Through the rear window's slope, the roadway's yellow lights beat an irregular pattern that I can almost distinguish through my closed eyes. The DeSoto's motor is the bass drone, the yellow lights are the rhythmic pulse, the voices on the radio – serial dramas like "My Little Margie" and "Bobby Benson and the B Bar B Riders" – form the melody lines.

My father likes to play guitar and sing. A sporadic student of Josh White – the blues master who left the Carolina Piedmont for a home in New York and engagements at Café Society – Manny gravitates to the folk music and union songs of Woody Guthrie and Pete Seeger. His guitar is a small nylon-string job, with inlay around the sound hole. "Cindy" is a family favorite

> *Get along home Cindy Cindy*
> *Get along home Cindy Cindy*
> *Get along home Cindy Cindy*
> *I'll marry you some day*

Years later, after we move to Boston and a house of our own, after I change my baseball allegiance from the Brooklyn Dodgers to the Red Sox, we name our collie after the song. We try to train her to come when we sing, but she never quite gets it, never quite understands that music is the family's subtext.

In Dorchester, on Boston's southern perimeter, I finish grade school and begin to attend Boston Latin School. The oldest public school in the country, it brags on its long history but, to my perspective, is showing its age. Boston Latin is considered superior to Boston Technical High School, which lives in the darker part of our segregated city, where students are expected to learn a manual trade rather than prepare for college. But that is where my mother takes me to hear my first gospel concert, headlined by Sister Rosetta Tharpe. Sister Rosetta is a shouter and a guitarist of epic strength. She sounds almost like the rock & roll that I am beginning to hear on the radio. Has she been listening to the Chuck Berry 45s that I carry in a tweed case and play on my one-speed Victrola? (Well no, the opposite makes more sense, when I can later construct a time-line.)

*Sister Rosetta Tharpe*

We're sitting in the center of the auditorium, not far from the stage. Sister Rosetta is building up a head of sacred steam, exhorting the crowd and half shouting her songs, when I hear a moan directly behind me, and then a commotion. I turn and see an elderly woman, her eyes weaving this way and that, seemingly disconnected from her brain and from each other. Her moans are interspersed with language far removed from English. Her arms flail spastically, and she looks like she's going to faint. She seems in trouble, and I am frightened for her. Why doesn't my mother react? No one around us seems bothered, either. In time – it seems like ages – two well-dressed attendants, calm and unfazed, walk to her side and proceed to caress her arms and fan her face. The spirit continues to possess this woman for some time, but eventually her movements grow less frantic, her voice less urgent. I can finally return my attention to the stage, where Sister Rosetta is urging us to lay down our sword and shield, down by the riverside. After a while, I turn and steal a glimpse at the agitated woman; she now sits in a peaceful glow, with a beatific smile across, maybe beyond, her face. Her eyes are focused now, but seemingly on a destination beyond this room.

A seed takes root with Paul Robeson's concert for children, and is fertilized by moments of musical understanding that Sister Rosetta Tharpe and others provide. But surely the plant blooms when my father undertakes a midlife career change by establishing Folklore Productions. In this new life, he becomes first a presenter of musical artists, and then their booker and manager. In this musical garden, I am nourished by a series of gifted mentors, whom these memories seek to honor and thank. They change my life by opening new ways of listening, and new ways of envisioning a future that would have, in their absence, been far different.

Decades later, when I am crossing into middle age, friends urge me to attend a one-man show about Paul Robeson, a theatrical recreation. But, because I still hold that fragile childhood memory of the man himself, I decline. I'm afraid that an actor, especially a good actor, will wipe it away, and the memory, like my firefly caged in a bottle, will fade and die.

Like the fireflies, musical moments of wonder shine before me, light my way, and illuminate my path from childhood to maturity. From each of my guides and mentors, I learn something about music, about myself, and about how a man carries himself in the world.

On my mind's desktop, I'm rummaging through some letters that, if I had been more perceptive, I might have written....

My "W.C. Handy" letter

## 13 YEARS OLD
### *Ice Skating with Pete Seeger*

My father has known Pete Seeger from a distance, through their days as labor activists in New York. And they were both in Peekskill, New York, around the time of my first concert experience, when Paul Robeson's audience was attacked by right-wing vigilantes. Now they have an appointment to meet formally, and Manny is excited at the prospect. He has a proposal to make to his hero.

In the summer of 1957 our family travels west, to Lenox, Massachusetts, where we attend a concert by Pete and the rest of the Weavers. At this point, the quartet – Pete Seeger, Lee Hayes, Ronnie Gilbert and Fred Hellerman – is several years removed from the days when its hit recordings of "Good Night Irene" and "Tzena Tzena" topped the pop music charts. And just about eighteen months past the sold out concert at Carnegie Hall that probably marked their peak as both artists and influences. If you're looking for the start of the folk revival, that's as good a marker as any.

After the concert, Manny and Pete have a long and serious conversation. My mother, my sister and I sit a few rows back from them in Lenox's barn auditorium, open to the steamy Berkshire summer that hovers just beyond the men's words. We listen as Pete explains that he has a problem: the McCarthy-era blacklist is

*The Weavers' most influential album*

causing local presenters to cancel confirmed bookings. He wants to find a New England presenter who will follow through, who will resist the pressure, who won't bail. "I'm your man," my father says, "I won't bail." He agrees to present Seeger's next Boston appearance.

Forty-five years later, as I am assembling a history of Folklore Productions, Pete responds to my letter with a phone call. He tries to remember the details. "I was reaching out, to give concerts in different cities," he recalls. As he talks, I picture Pete at the other end of the phone line. I see him in classic Pete pose, head cocked slightly to the right, focusing on some imaginary object in his middle dis-

## 13 YEARS OLD: ICE SKATING WITH PETE SEEGER

*Advertising Pete Seeger*

*FBI file on Manny Greenhill.*

tance field, as he recalls Manny making the commitment to stand up to the pressure that both knew would be coming.

These concerns are well founded. Some months later, with the concert booked and advertised, an FBI agent accosts my dad at the Butler Street trolley stop, on his way to work. After identifying himself, the agent asks why Folklore Productions is presenting Pete Seeger, a known Communist sympathizer, in concert. Despite a growing inner panic – our family knows many who have lost their jobs to the Red Scare – Manny shrugs to cover his nervousness. "He sells tickets," is his reply, as, feigning nonchalance, he returns to his crossword puzzle.

After my father's death in 1996, I request his FBI files, and find that someone in our Dorchester neighborhood had been talking to the FBI, informing on the comings and goings to and from our home at 4 Huntoon Street. The bureau knew much about our household, and was protecting the republic by keeping a watchful eye. "Boston informants have been unable to identify GREENHILL in connection with Communist Party affairs in the area," reads a typical passage, "and extended surveillances on the subject's place of business and his residence disclose no significant activity." The report is "classified Confidential because it contains information from concealed sources of continuing value, the identities of whom would impair their future usefulness to the prejudice of the security interests of the United States." It further notes that the subject of surveillance "was thoroughly uncooperative."

A few weeks after the encounter at the trolley stop, with the concert just hours away, Pete takes me ice-skating. He is our houseguest now, along with blues harmonica virtuoso Sonny Terry, who will visit frequently in the years to follow, and Sonny's nephew J.C. Burris, who, after starting out as their driver, winds up playing bones in the concert.

It's not a formal skating rink, with manicured ice and a rail to mark its boundaries. Rather, it's a temporary play area in the neighborhood tradition – when the weather turns cold, the fire department opens a hydrant near a low stretch of marshland, to form an ice pond for winter. The ice is rough and uneven. Bushes jut out from beneath its surface. At one end sits a small wooden cabin, heated to provide respite from the New England winter.

*An informal ice rink*

To tell the truth, I am not much of an ice skater, and I'm quite sensitive to cold weather. So I usually spend at least as much time in the cabin, hunkered next to the heat, as I do on the ice. But today I'm following Pete Seeger, the pied piper of song, who loves the ice and seems impervious to the cold. He leans his lanky frame into graceful turns around the bushes. His scarf trails in his breezy wake, and an equally colorful wool cap protects his thinning hair.

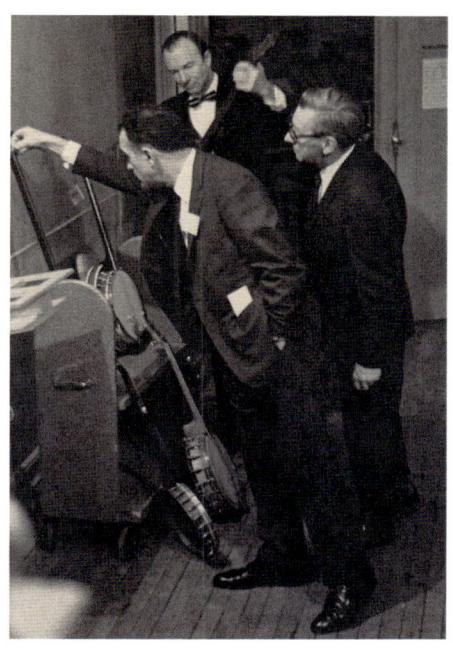

*Manny and Pete backstage*

I struggle to keep up, and actually make some progress. I don't feel as cold as usual, and at times, emulating Pete, I almost seem to feel the rhythm of ice-skating.

An early lesson: Find the rhythm. Brave the cold. Balance.

Back home, it is more excitement than our little corner of Dorchester is used to. Pete's banjo rings through the rooms, and one afternoon a University of Massachusetts student, a tall young black man who calls himself Taj Mahal, takes a break from his studies in Animal Husbandry to stop by and pay his respects. (I will eventually become Taj's booking agent, but that's a quarter century into the future; for now we are both trying to digest the new musical banquet laid before us.)

The concert is wonderful, and a big success. Sitting in the audience, I find it thrilling, even empowering, to harmonize labor songs with Pete. He has a compelling way of leading a group of people while at the same time submerging himself into one part of a larger whole. It's magical to be both his follower and his singing companion. Plus his instrumental chops are formidable – we hear both the high sparkle of his longneck banjo and the low rumble of his twelve-string guitar. As an added bonus, he brings out a big axe and chops an actual log on stage while singing a work song. Nor does he disappoint those who expect a political critique: at one point he has us all singing that we will own the banks made of marble. And when he leads us in Woody Guthrie's "This Land Is Your Land," he includes the verse about the sign that says "private property" on one side, but nothing on the other side, and concludes, "That side was made for you and me."

Pete is a door to a new world, a world in which we live as we sing, in harmony. A world in which injustices are addressed and made right. A world held together by common interests, and by music. I want to live in that world.

*Two-year-old Pete Seeger with family*

And staid Jordan Hall, home to the august New England Conservatory of Music, is sold out. "The blacklist gave me a lot of free publicity," Seeger will tell me years later.

Pete returns to our house a number of times. He usually brings Toshi and the kids: Dan, Tinya and Mika. At times the house seems to be bursting with Seegers. One time Pete brings his mother, who warns us against the evils of chlorinated water.

Many years later, after I join my father in the business, and especially after Dan's wife Martha begins to work as Manny's assistant, Pete and Toshi will stop by the office in Santa Monica. We walk to the Santa Monica Pier for a lunch of crab sandwiches. Pete allows himself a beer, and then, uncharacteristically, another. In the afternoon's sunny breeze, he reminisces about his father, folklorist Charles Seeger, who showed him the path to traditional music. Toshi thinks that Charles developed a machine to more accurately render the vocal decorations and mannerisms of the old-time singers, and she wonders if it may be in a basement at UCLA, a few miles away.

*Mitch, Katie Down, Matt Darriau, Pete, Matt Greenhill at the Clearwater Festival*

We never get around to exploring that lead. But we do get to UCLA in another way: that's where we return to the company's roots by presenting Pete Seeger yet again. This time the co-bill is not Sonny Terry, but rather Reverend James Cleveland and his powerful gospel choir.

The last time I see Pete, we are at Brooklyn College, observing Woody Guthrie's 100th birthday with a concert that includes the Klezmatics, whom I now manage. At this point, Toshi is confined to a wheelchair, and Pete and Tinya take turns wheeling her, much as she used to wheel baby Dan around Washington Square Park. As he does virtually every time that our paths cross, Pete remembers ice-skating with me, and marvels that I look different than I did in 1957.

If music is a calling, it is Pete, as much as anybody, who calls me. But he is not the only one. He is, rather, first in a series.

In the years to come, other powerful musicians will sleep in our guest room, eat my mother's pot roast, and most crucially play music on the living room couch. One song that sticks with me is the gospel piece about looking back and wondering "how I got over." To the extent that I ever do "get over," it is due in large part to what these influential artists are willing to share with an inquisitive teenager who wants nothing more than to hear what they are hearing, to comprehend their compelling melodies and tempos, to get inside the music.

## A SURROGATE UNCLE, AND WHAT THE WELL-DRESSED MUSICIAN WILL WEAR

"Listen," Steve Gardner tells my parents, "you raise your kid the way you want to," – here, like the good story-teller he is, he pauses for effect – "and I'll raise him the way I want to." The argument under discussion – some aspect of my transgressive behavior, no doubt, and Steve's subversive encouragement – yields to involuntary chuckles. His role as my parents' friend and my surrogate uncle once again smooths the rough abrasions of teenage life. Steve can hear and be heard by both sides.

We're surely discussing some marginally appropriate room that Steve has walked me into. Maybe Blinstrub's nightclub in South Boston, where Eartha Kitt gives a performance more sexually explicit than this thirteen-year-old knows what to do with. She vamps and struts her curves in a come-hither way that confuses and embarrasses me. But not Steve. When I glance his way, he is enjoying himself immensely, grinning and chuckling knowingly. He's keeping me out past my curfew, but it's okay – he's raising me his way.

Once he walks me into the Union Oyster House, which has been purveying New England seafood for well over a century. As we enter, I nearly trip over a live lobster, who has somehow crawled out of the big tank by the door and is attempting a feverish, futile escape. Perhaps it's the same lobster that we later dig into, as Steve shows me the proper way to crack the shell, use the little fork, dip the meat in butter, and, most importantly, how to wear the mandatory bib while maintaining the *savoir-faire* and flair of a proletarian *bon vivant*. "Follow me, kid," is Steve's unspoken invitation. "If I can keep up," I tell myself.

For a while it's hard to know where Steve lives, exactly. He spends time in our guest room. And there are times when, as a professional stage manager, he's out on the road with a touring theatrical production. Sometimes these coincide: when *The Tenth Man* plays Boston, Steve and his girlfriend, an understudy in the production, stay with us.

But in a real sense, the racetrack – Belmont Park or Aqueduct or Saratoga Race Course – is his true home. That's where Steve's blacklisted writer friends eke out a living when the networks won't hire them. Some use Steve as a "front," the guy who has not been blacklisted, so can sell scripts under his own or an assumed name. When he takes me to the track, Steve introduces me to Harry the Horse and other tipsters. The track is Steve's neighborhood, his social scene. And eventually his ashes will lie under the turf, at Saratoga's quarter pole.

But he can't sleep at the track, so eventually he rents an apartment on Bank Street in Greenwich Village. When I somehow find myself spending a weekend there, Steve's tutorial, now freed from any parental restraints, moves into high gear. After a few instructions on proper coffee etiquette and how to season pasta sauce, we bundle ourselves against the winter wind and trudge several blocks to the Village Vanguard, a dark and resonant jazz cabaret on Seventh Avenue. Along the way, Steve spins an emblematic story of his history with the place, where he used to work as stage manager. In an experimental break from its jazz programing, owner Max Gordon has hired the Weavers, with Pete Seeger on banjo. For the Weavers it represents a professional breakthrough from singing at

*"Uncle" Steve Gardner*

union rallies to becoming the first truly popular band of city folk singers. The initial booking is extended for an additional week, then more, until they become almost the house band.

As Steve tells it, Max Gordon is paying the Weavers $50 per singer per week. But he supplements the modest salary by giving the artists relatively free rein in the kitchen. Specifically, each of the four Weavers is allowed to make one sandwich from ingredients stocked in the larder. Three of the Weavers keep their appetites within reasonable parameters, but Pete is accused of violating the spirit, if not the letter, of the agreement by building immense towers of sandwich architecture, perhaps the only full meal of his day.

Max Gordon, seeing his profits going down the thin Seeger skeleton and seeing few paying customers feeding the till, decides to fire the band. With relish, Steve relives his heroic role in negotiating the crucial pact between labor and management that saves the booking. The Vanguard and the Weavers digest the agreement and prosper.

*What the well-dressed musician wears – early Miles*

*What the well-dressed musician wears – late Miles*

*What the well-dressed musician wears – Pete Seeger*

In later years, I'll crosscheck this tale with Pete. "Some nights only four people would show up," he tells me, "And we would forget the microphones. Instead, we would sit around tables with the audience and sing informally." Pete recalls living a few blocks from the Vanguard, off Washington Square. He allows that on some nights he probably spirited half the sandwich back home, to share with wife Toshi and baby Dan, who in later years will become my friend. (Rather than his father's ice-skating, Dan Seeger and I will bond over scuba-diving.) In the mornings, Pete recalls, Toshi would leave early, so that Pete could sleep off the previous night's exertions. That's when she would push Dan's carriage around Washington Square Park, where on weekends the park's fountain would be surrounded by a new generation of folk singers, learning songs and trading licks.

Steve and I arrive at the Vanguard, and navigate the steep flight of stairs down into the basement concert room. It takes me a few minutes to adjust to the dim lighting and make out the black-and-white photos on the burgundy wall, a pantheon of jazz luminaries. There's not a guitar or banjo in sight, but instead a quintet – trumpet, saxophone, piano, bass and drums – is weaving a confusing musical tapestry on the bandstand.

Steve says hello to Max and his old buddies, and suggests that I pay attention to the trumpet player, a certain Miles Davis. Davis is wearing a suit, not the work shirt and dungarees that Pete Seeger has accustomed me to. Where Seeger treats me and the rest of the audience like his best friends, Davis turns his back to us. He's letting me observe his communion with a musical muse, but does not welcome or explain. I'm on my own. This different brand of musical sorcery rattles around my head, as if looking for a place to set down roots. If there's a structure to this music, it eludes me.

Where is the verse? Where is the chorus? Nobody in the audience is singing along.

Davis finishes his solo and John Coltrane takes over. I'll see the saxophonist again, a few years later, when I attend an all-ages matinee at Boston's Jazz Workshop. There I'm part of a full house, all of us too young for the evening, alcohol-laced main gig, nervously waiting for Coltrane to arrive and perform. I order a Coke, then another, and wonder if I should leave. But no, I've paid my admission and am determined to see it through. After maybe an hour, one or two band members begin to drift onto the stage. The drummer smokes a cigarette as he adjusts the tension on his snare. Some anxious minutes later, John Coltrane walks through the front door and elbows his way through the teenage crowd to the bandstand, where he calmly and deliberately unpacks his horn. Barely pausing to moisten his reed, he unleashes a torrent of notes, the famous "wall of sound," that continues, virtually uninterrupted, for about an hour. Like Miles, he doesn't talk to the people. When he has completed his musical statement, Coltrane packs his horn, walks through the crowd, and is gone.

John Coltrane still wears a suit. But Miles Davis's stage clothing will evolve over the course of his career. When I last see him, shortly before his death, he is wearing custom crafted outfits of shiny fabrics with fringe and eye-popping patterns. Pete Seeger, on the other hand, pretty much sticks to work clothes. What he wears on stage is not that different from what he wears at home, chopping wood.

At the Village Vanguard, Coltrane finishes his solo and the band ratchets up the intensity. I'm wearing Seeger-style clothes, a flannel shirt and chinos. On Monday, when I return to Boston Latin School, I'll have to abide by its dress code and wear a tie at all times. I'll obey, but make sure that I also wear a flannel work shirt, like Pete Seeger. To each system, its own rebellious gestures.

The set ends and the patrons file up the narrow stairway to Seventh Avenue. I watch as Miles Davis and John Coltrane pack up their horns and leave the Village Vanguard. I see "Uncle" Steve at the bar, wrapping up one of his stories. After a punch line and some laughter, he bundles me into my overcoat and we walk the few blocks back to his apartment on Bank Street. He has again taken me to a new place at the edge of what I can comprehend. And again, I feel at once safe, adventurous and disoriented.

# 14 YEARS OLD
## *Theory and Practice with Rolf Cahn*

In 1958 Rolf Cahn arrives at our house. He stays for several months, a long time, even by our relaxed standards. Soon he is contributing to the household by teaching me guitar, and thus offering a better alternative – especially as it must seem to my parents – to my hanging out, bored, on street corners. Rolf becomes something of a guide, accompanying my precarious transition to manhood.

He is noticeably different from anyone I've ever met. I'm intrigued and a bit frightened at his intensity. Short, muscular, his hat at a rakish angle, a half-smoked cigar dangling from his lips, he spins stories of early years as a Jewish boy in Germany, as Hitler is rising to power. At one point, fixing his laser stare at me, he describes a Nuremburg rally as he heard it broadcast and announced on radio: loud, intense buildup until the stadium is full. Bands play, German youth march, dignitaries appear by the dozen. And then: "The powerful climax – Hitler walks out in silence, alone." Here Rolf gives

*Rolf Cahn*

# 14 YEARS OLD: THEORY AND PRACTICE WITH ROLF CAHN

November 24, 1958
9522 Halldale
Los Angeles, Calif.

Mr. M. A. Greenhill
P.O. Box 227
Boston, Mass.

Dear Mr. Greenhill;

You have been recommended by friends as the key person for professional activity in Folk Music in the Boston area. I'm anxious to find out how I could sustain myself there for a few months before going to Europe. I can offer the following things to the community:

    CONCERTS---I have concertized out here successfully since 1952, both in Folk Music and Flamenco. A tape of a very recent composite concert is available to you through Miss Molly Scott, at Smith College.

    WORKSHOP & LECTURES---Recent lectures include these subjects:
        The musical esthetics of folk music, basically an approach to compare, and at times contrast, to composed European music.
        The urban folk-song community, it's history, present situation, and direction---this is a discussion of "us".
        The music of the Negro People in the United States, an expansion of the lecture series of the Negro Spiritual
        Flamenco---description and demonstration of the music of Andalucia and neighboring provinces.
        The Guitar---a workshop for instrumentalists and teachers to share my experience in playing and teaching the instrument.

    GUITAR LESSONS---I have been teaching the Spanish guitar since 1952. My method is basically oriented toward folk music, with wide and necessary excursions into theory, scales, and technique adapted from classic guitar, although I do not play or teach classic guitar. Over the years, I have developed a comprehensive method for teaching which includes American techniques (Blues, Rhythms, Carter Family picking, finger-picking) Carribbean and Spanish American techniques, a general approach to accompaniment, and a thorough method in Flamenco. Odetta Phelious mentioned that Mr. Saletan is no longer teaching, and that there was a possibility of his former students being without an instructor.

Let me apologize for presumption in expounding such a program in a first communication. Thank you very much for your consideration.

                                      Sincerely yours,

                                      Rolf Cahn

*Rolf introduces himself to Manny*

his distinct giggle, or maybe a cackle, at the wicked absurdity of the times. I've heard a few Hitler stories, but until now, they were never laugh lines. And never came from one so close to the action.

During World War II he returned to Europe, parachuting behind enemy lines for the OSS and blowing up bridges. "I killed people," he recalls, this time without laughter. I find the story – and especially the mood swing – sobering.

Rolf sings the blues with a guttural German accent. It's quite a while before I realize that this is not how they talk in the Mississippi Delta.

He sings and plays flamenco, which he studied in Granada, with a similar accent. He attacks the flamenco guitar aggressively, pounding the strings with his right hand, beating them into submission.

He talks of his time in prison. He's vague about why or where, but clear that he developed a love of boxing there. He describes his passion for the sport in lyrical, almost musical terms – its rhythms, its cadences, its tensions and resolutions. And then finally, "It's almost a shame that you have to hit the man."

He romances a series of archetypal blond *shiksas*. When I first meet him, it is Molly Scott, who comes to town in a quasi-theatrical revue called "3 Folk Sing." Before that, Barbara Dane, the formidable blues singer, mother of his son Jesse. Later, when our guitar lessons move to his apartment in Cambridge, it is Debbie Green, who recognized a kindred spirit in Joan Baez on their first day at Boston University, when both – along with Betsy Siggins, soon to become a powerful force at Club 47's burgeoning music scene – refused to wear freshman beanie caps.

And still later, when I am on the road as a traveling musician, performing in Berkeley, he invites me to join a few close friends in his apartment, where yet another blond woman, Bobbie, gives loud painful birth in the next room. Her screams cut through the California sunset for hours, a sound I've never heard before. I'm frightened for her, want that sound to stop and wish that the baby

*Debbie Green and Rolf at home in Cambridge*

would come already, let us move out of this excruciating limbo. But Bobbie is determined to deliver naturally, without drugs. Rolf paces and worries; he is all for an epidural.

At last, deep in the night, the baby arrives, healthy. Bobbie too is fine, and we join them in the bedroom. I learn that Rolf is not the biological father, but wants to take responsibility, be there for mother and child. Hearing the newborn's first cry, someone says "Score one cherub." At this Rolf lets go of his anxiety and gives his unique characteristic cackle. "Hipster poetry," he beams, loving the phrase.

To Rolf, these romances – blond WASPS partnering with a European Jewish hipster – have a somewhat political cast, the culmination of a caste war against square America. "We take their women!" is his victory cry.

But most important to me, Rolf knows his way around a guitar neck and the instrument's history. He drills me in solos of the greats, including Sister Rosetta Tharpe, whom I recall from that concert in Boston. Rolf shows me how Sister Rosetta makes those pre-Chuck Berry sounds – the fingers on her left hand form double-stops as her right thumb hits two strings at one time. Then she moves them up or down the fret board, the two lines moving in harmony. A revelation!

Rolf says that I have an aptitude for the instrument, and he's eager to impart his catechism. My progress is exciting for both of us. I want to please him, and he keeps setting the bar higher, leading me into more complex and sophisticated material.

Rolf has a philosophy, an intellectual fervor, about guitar pedagogy, as he does about pretty much everything. When my father suggests that classical guitar instruction is the best way to start – and, in fact, I eventually do take some lessons in that discipline, from one Guy Simeone, at whose urging I attend a concert by Andrés Segovia – Rolf is horrified. "Oh no," he declares, "The techniques are completely different. And when Maestro Simeone, making a similar argument from the other side, declares that I must give up the blues in order to really learn classical guitar, I move into Rolf's camp with barely a backwards glance.

Hoping to please Maestro Cahn, I practice guitar assiduously and read the books he recommends (like *The Horn*, by John Clellon Holmes). When he tells me, "You won't be able to truly play the blues until you truly believe that you will die someday," I entertain morbid fantasies, imagining my demise many times over, trying to internalize the experience. Will I ever get inside this music? I'll do anything – what will it take?

When a lesson concludes without my having mastered what has been taught, the subway ride home finds me frustrated and discouraged. The train is tightly packed with a thick slab of Boston's varied but usually isolated groups – students toting bookbags to or from their dormitories, ladies carrying shopping bags back to the southern suburbs, wimpled nuns, workers with lunch pails, businessmen with briefcases. I stand, a subway strap in one hand, my guitar in the other, focused on something else. Internally, I enter

# 14 YEARS OLD: THEORY AND PRACTICE WITH ROLF CAHN

a feverish reverie, going over Rolf's lesson, seeing his hands, following how they move. Then I envision my own wayward fingers, and compel them to follow Rolf's lead, to etch his sonic pathway into my resistant synapses. And when I arrive home and unpack my guitar, sometimes I find myself suddenly able to play what I have been envisioning. Maybe I have more capacity than I thought.

*Rolf Cahn*

Sensing a need to go deeper, Rolf approaches one lesson from a different angle. Instead of listening to how well I've mastered last week's lesson and then moving on to a new piece of music, he asks about my romantic life. At fourteen, I barely have any, but I do have a mass of hormonal frustrations, back seat necking and petting sessions, problems understanding how to unhook a bra strap with one hand. I've never told these embarrassments to anyone, but now they all rush forth. I trust Rolf, like no one else, not to make fun of my emotions, not to make me seem foolish.

He listens, nodding sympathetically. Sometime during my tale of angst he puts the guitar in my hand and asks me to play the blues. I hesitate at first, but then, quietly at first, I begin to play. I immediately feel a different connection to the music and to the instrument. The power of connection, between my emotions and my musical expression, surprises and comforts me.

I play for quite a while and with a new intensity. When I stop, I'm exhausted. Rolf smiles approvingly and observes, "We do so much for the love of woman." I feel protected by an aura of understanding that lasts through the subway ride back to Dorchester, the walk uphill past the piles of smoldering autumn leaves, and on into the night.

Not long after, Rolf at last asks me to accompany him in concert. It takes place on a real stage, in a real concert hall, just around the corner from Symphony Hall, center of Boston's high culture. There are lights and a sound system.

Rolf begins with a few solo pieces, then introduces me. I walk on stage, and try a few approaches to the microphone. Rolf has begun an introduction to the next song, but I'm not really following him. Instead I'm looking out into the dark audience, shading my eyes from the stage lights. I'm wondering when I should start playing and how will I know? We never practiced that part. Meanwhile Rolf's remarks are going down well with the audience, eliciting some knowing hip laughter. He's taking forever, and I'm hopping up and down on the balls of my feet, barely containing myself. Eventually he nods at me, a signal to begin. I attack the guitar strings as if striking a heavy gong, and we're off. I'm standing with Rolf Cahn as a peer. It seems as if, in a sense, I have graduated.

As time goes on, Rolf's aura tarnishes a bit. I notice that he lives in a state of near-constant paranoia. The war may be over for the United States and its allies, but for Rolf, not really. He is especially nervous around marijuana. I wonder, is this what sent him to prison years ago, where he learned to box?

Some six or seven years after my graduation concert, I'm a college student, eager to show Rolf my first off-campus apartment. It's a small place, but I've tried to make it homey by putting the couch low to the floor, to hide that we are really in the kitchen. Rolf sinks into the couch and rolls a joint. We light up and he goes off onto one of his philosophical riffs, theorizing exuberantly in a cloud of smoke. Suddenly he stops, realizing that only a thin wall separates us from the apartment next door. "Can they hear us?" he whispers. "Do they know we are smoking?" The mood changes as his defenses bristle, even though this is Cambridge in the mid

*Rolf and contraband*

1960s, and probably every apartment on the street is equipped with a stash and a pipe.

Years later – after publication of his book, *Self Defense For Gentle People* – I visit him in Santa Fe. He now earns his living by chainsawing big limbs to place artfully in yuppie living rooms, places that inspire his contempt. His defenses are still on hair-trigger alert. Before sharing some high-grade reefer, we first retreat into what now seems a safe room, a bunker even, soundproof and without windows. He locks the door, and at last eases into his own imitation of relaxation. And this time there is no next-door apartment, nobody to hear us, nobody to know we're smoking.

As time passes and I acquired other mentors, Rolf's glamour continues to fade. He seems too didactic, too uptight, too cerebral. In later years, when I am approaching middle age and he is leaving it, he asks me to accompany him on a couple of concerts in Los Angeles. The first of these is a modest success – about 40 people attend and enthusiastically receive the music. A memorable party follows, highlighted by a surprise appearance by The Chambers Brothers. This makes a big impression on our hostess. "No, you don't understand," she feverishly tells her husband, "The Chambers Brothers are HERE in OUR HOUSE!" Rolf shrugs and cackles. "Joe Chambers has white hair!" he giggles.

At this point, Rolf is no longer playing blues or flamenco. He has, rather, fashioned himself into a singer-songwriter. But to my more mature ears, his new songs are, frankly, not that good. The melodies are derivative. And the lyrics celebrate a "special love" that seems to come unnaturally from the ironic and rigorous mentor who used to critique any shred of easy sentiment. When he leaves town after the concert, I feel it's the end of this chapter. I don't feel the need to follow up my graduation with Rolfian post-graduate studies.

Then, a year or two later, he comes back and he again asks me to accompany him. But by now I'm no longer waiting for him to ask me to play. Now I have other musical projects, and a family, and a cold. This time I decline. "Sorry man," I beg off, "I have this nasty cold and need to hunker down, drink some tea." He accepts my explanation gracefully enough, but over the phone line I can hear a change in his voice, one that today fills me with regret. In retrospect, it seems wrong. While my sniffles were real, were they insurmountable? As a teenager, I would have left any sickbed, no matter how serious my condition, to grab the opportunity. Apologies, Rolf, I should have been there for you.

I imagine that concert now, the one I should not have missed. I take the stage behind my old mentor, and listen to the chord changes as intently as I did when a young student. When he nods, I take a solo, concise and fully in the spirit of the musical moment. As the concert concludes, in my imagination it is enthusiastically received, and Rolf is basking in the audience's approval. I take a few steps back, to leave him the spotlight and the attention. In my mind's eye, I see him happy and fulfilled.

    A few years later, liver cancer takes Rolf and his music, his antic personality and his restless mind. I wish I had said a better good-bye.

*I will take my last journey in this land somewhere*
*I will take my last journey in this land somewhere*
*I don't know where I will be, maybe out on the ocean, way out on the sea*
*I will take my last journey in this land somewhere*
— *Reverend Gary Davis*

## 4 HUNTOON STREET, DORCHESTER LOWER MILLS
*A Parade of Musical Visitors*

Our house sits on a corner lot. Up a rise and to the left stands Baker's Chocolate Mill, whose sweet odor permeates the neighborhood. Or so we are told by visitors; we residents don't notice it.

*When I was young, I lived by the chocolate mill*
*And the smell of that sweetness would drift on down the hill*

Down the hill and to the right is the trolley stop, where my dad leaves for work, and where that FBI agent confronted him about Pete Seeger. Beyond lie the Neponset River's wetlands, which our cat explores in communion with her jungle ancestors. On the other side of the river, just outside the Boston city limits, the leafy suburbs begin.

*I would wait for a trolley by an endless track*
*To be taken away and never look back*
*Part of me is still the boy by the chocolate mill*

The front door leads to a hallway, with the kitchen at its end. To the right, a stairway leads to bedrooms. First the guest room. That's where Pete Seeger stays when he takes me ice-skating, and where Rolf Cahn lives while teaching me guitar. Across the hall is my sister's room. Then, as the hall makes a right-angle turn, the master bedroom. And finally my room, in the far corner next to the bathroom. Any musical guest heading to the john needs to go past my room.

Downstairs is a big living room with a generous couch, the home's musical center, and a piano. There is a dining room, an enclosed porch that gets pretty cold in winter, and a substantial back yard with a rocky ledge over the street corner and a scraggly crabapple tree.

Manny and Leona Greenhill are around forty years old when we move into this, the first home that they have ever owned. It is a real house, not an apartment or a typical Boston three-decker, with a family on each level. We lived in one of those a few years ago, in Winthrop, just across the street from the ocean sea wall. During storms, waves from the Atlantic would leap up over the concrete barrier and across the street, and would rap on our windows, like a soggy drum roll. And before that, ever since their marriage in 1941, a few months after meeting at a May Day parade, they lived in apartments, like the one in Brooklyn, where I chased fireflies.

Although she enjoys a good joke, my mom is the sterner, more severe parent. She disciplines my sister and me, and provides a strict moral compass to the entire household, including Manny. He is looser, more likely to splurge on (and indulge in) a better brand of Scotch. (Leona sips a single glass of sherry before dinner.) But when issues arise of social justice for workers and minority groups, Manny assumes a sterner demeanor. Once, when in an attempt to look hip I dress myself entirely in black, he gets very angry and comes down on me hard. It reminds him of Mussolini's blackshirts and the struggle against fascism that first radicalized him, back in the 1930s. Hurt and tearful, I don't understand. My mother, the peacemaker, talks him down. What does a kid know from Mussolini?

This political fervor is what connects him first to Pete Seeger and later to Joan Baez. Political discussions animate the dinner table, and my parents' friends, especially those who visit from New York, contain a number of blacklisted victims of the era's Red Scare, which is just beginning to wind down. Manny has managed to reconcile his sensual appetites with his Marxism by deciding that nothing's too good for the working class. He keeps bottles of champagne in the fridge for special moments, and these seem to arise so frequently that their celebratory signature would be erased, except for the sense of occasion that accompanies the popping of each cork.

Although few if any of our Dorchester neighbors share our household's left-wing views, they are actual members of the working class. My dad used to be a manual laborer, including a stretch in steel mills, but these days he works at a desk. Most of Huntoon Street is Irish, with the occasional Pole and Italian. One friend's sister becomes a nun; another's father works for the fire department, inspecting houses. All are loyal Democrats. The neighborhood, Dorchester Lower Mills, lies just inside the city limits. Across the Neponset River lies Milton, a Republican bastion of manicured lawns and substantial homes, some of them more like estates. Lower Mills, on our side of the river, resists suburbia, maintains its hardscrabble city identity.

On that first visit with Pete Seeger, my family and Sonny Terry become friends. The following year Sonny returns as our house guest and visiting artist. Manny has partnered with jazz impresario George Wein to start a new club, The Ballad Room, in the Copley Square Hotel, just downstairs from Wein's Storyville. While Storyville is an established jazz venue, The Ballad Room will present folk music, now rapidly gaining popularity among college audiences.

The Ballad Room will mark its inauguration by presenting the first Boston appearance of Sonny Terry & Brownie McGhee. The harmonica-guitar duo, already pretty well known in New York's folk music scene, is now beginning to venture farther afield.

The performance is already being promoted with print advertisements and radio spots, when an awkward problem arises. A new coffee shop near Boston University, called the Golden Vanity, moves in to take advantage of the blues duo's presence in the area. The Golden Vanity wants to present Sonny & Brownie several days before their appearance at The Ballad Room. Manny objects to this cut-price competition, and I am, for the first of many times, torn between family and a would-be peer group. The Vanity is hip, cutting edge, and I want to be accepted there. I can dream of performing on its simple wooden stage. At least once a week, I ride there on the subway, including two changes of trains, to hear music, drink fruity beverages with exotic names like "grenadine," and soak in the knowing, collegiate atmosphere.

---

*Sonny Terry is the first, but by no means the last blind artist to stay at our home. As the years go on, we will meet Reverend Gary Davis, Doc Watson and others. But being the first, Sonny becomes our teacher.*

*Years later, Doc Watson gives me a formal lesson on how to lead a blind person. "Just give me your elbow," he says, "And go straight. Walk just like normal, and I'll follow. When you go up or down a stair, I'll know." One night I knock on Doc's hotel room door and, after he lets me in, I express surprise that all the lights are off, the room in darkness. That sets Doc to musing how it might indeed be more considerate to the "sighted person" if he remembers to turn the lights on. Who is leading whom, I wonder?*

*Reverend Gary Davis, more aggressively confronting his blindness, writes a chilling song titled "There Was a Time That I Went Blind," which he calls "The darkest day that I ever saw."*

*Sonny Terry & Brownie McGhee*

As I'm starting to expand my horizons out into the wider world, the Golden Vanity is an early destination.

Eventually a compromise is reached: rather than presenting the duo, the Vanity will present only Sonny Terry, without Brownie McGhee. Instead, Sonny will be accompanied by Eric von Schmidt, who has recently returned from a year in Rome on a Fulbright scholarship in painting. There he also growled the blues at the legendary club Bricktops. He's been playing some local gigs with Rolf Cahn, and I've been eager to hear and to get to know him. And since Sonny is our houseguest, my job – and my first apprenticeship to Folklore Productions, a company I will eventually inherit – is to be a helpful companion to the blind harmonica virtuoso, see that his needs are met.

Meanwhile, The Ballad Room will retain its distinction as first Boston presenter of the duo, Sonny Terry & Brownie McGhee.

As we prepare to leave, my mother looks in the downstairs closet and asks Sonny what color is his coat. The blind harmonica player chuckles at her oversight and says, "It's the biggest one." Flustered, she remarks on his positive attitude in the face of his handicap. "Would it help if I cried?" he asks.

My dad drives us to The Golden Vanity and moves on to prepare his own club for its opening night. He'll pick us up at the end of the evening.

The Golden Vanity has been decked out in nautical gear, as befits the ballad that has inspired its name. Heavy ropes tied in improbable knots form a backdrop to the stage, and instead of tables, the audience is seated around wooden barrels. No one seems to notice the negative connotations of the ballad's last verse:

*Sonny Terry*

*One time around spun our gallant ship*
*Two times around spun she*
*Three times around spun our gallant ship*
*And she sank to the bottom of the sea*

Upstairs, in the dressing room, a none-too-sober Eric von Schmidt and a more restrained Sonny Terry struggle to feel their way through planning a set. They have never met, but hey, it's a tiny folk music club in the late 1950's, and no one seems to be feeling any pressure.

Or maybe the tension is subliminal. Eric quickly works his way through a pint of dark rum. Finding it empty, he tosses it out the window, and we hear it shatter on the sidewalk below.

Onstage, the new duo somehow manages to pull it off. The crowd loves Sonny's ribald songs, with *double entendres* that go over my adolescent head. I can't understand the big laughter at a blues that describes a man coming home and learning that "that key you got, Sonny Terry, won't fit my lock no more." And then he opines that a skinny-legged woman is good for only one thing – to go get him a big-legged woman, with "meat shaking on her bones." To Sonny's harmonica accompaniment, Eric sings an original blues about a street in Washington:

> *P Street's on fire, the whole town's burning down*
> *P Street's on fire, the whole town's burning down*
> *These P Street women just call for another round.*

The Golden Vanity is launched. Unlike the ship in the ballad, this vessel survives and flourishes for several years.

Some days later and some miles away, The Ballad Room opens with its own strengths and charms. At the bottom of a flight of stairs, its dark walls feature Eric von Schmidt's original oil paintings of Jelly Roll Morton and Jimmy Yancey, drawn from feel as Eric listens to their music, rather than from photographs or contemporary descriptions. The main room looks more like a traditional nightclub, a smaller version of Blinstrub's, where Eartha Kitt confused me a year or so earlier. The audience tends to dress up, and they are drinking alcoholic beverages, not fruit drinks and coffee. The dressing room is the hotel's barber shop, and guitar players have a hard time holding and tuning their instruments as they navigate the barber chairs' arm rests and swivels.

Joan Baez plays Club 47, over in Cambridge, only two nights a week. Can she and Manny come to an agreement about playing The Ballad Room on other nights? His

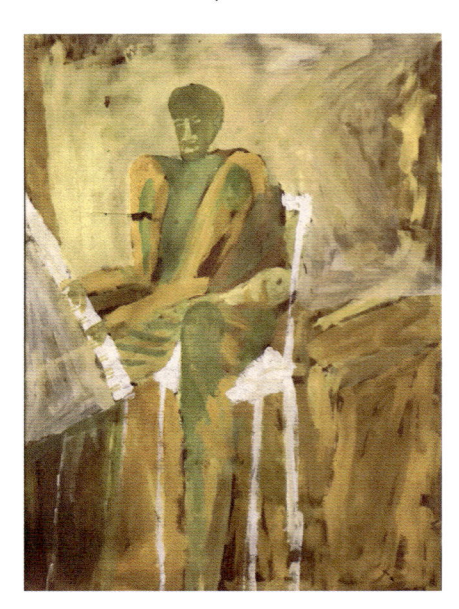

*Jimmy Yancey, by Eric von Schmid*

> **GEORGE WEIN & MANUEL GREENHILL**
>
> *announce the opening of*
>
> # the Ballad Room
>
> *New England's only night club devoted to folk music and related forms of entertainment*
>
> (Opened — October 8th)
>
> *featuring*
> - BUD & TRAVIS
> - ROLF CAHN
>
> *Exeter Street off Huntington Avenue, Boston
> downstairs at Copley Square Hotel*

*The Ballad Room, early advertisement*

partner George Wein later recalls her holding out for more money. "She said, 'I'm getting 25; he doesn't want to pay me 30 dollars.' I says, 'we'll give you 30 dollars a night.' She says, 'Okay.' I mean, that's what life was in those days."

As Manny's son, I have free access, and I take full advantage. After Sonny Terry & Brownie McGhee's appearance, the New Lost City Ramblers come for a week's engagement. Then Barbara Dane, Rolf Cahn's ex-wife, arrives, accompanied by Memphis Slim and Willie Dixon, who also play their own set. Willie takes a liking to me, shows me some blues subtleties, and tells stories of the Chicago scene.

Willie is a big man, with massive hands. He wields his double bass like a small tool. His right hand makes a rhythmic slap on the backbeat, while his left hand makes the neck look like a guitar neck. He has a big spirit, as well, with a welcoming *joie de vivre* that encourages me, draws me out.

Memphis Slim is quieter, reflective – more Miles Davis to Willie's Pete Seeger. He communes with the piano as if at a séance, as if contacting a far-off world that only he can hear. "I don't care how great you are," he sings, "I don't care what you're worth – When it all ends up, you got to go back to Mother Earth." Following Rolf's lessons on the relationship between death and the blues, I'm beginning to have a hazy notion of what he invokes. Decades later I will attend his funeral in Memphis, where he is lowered into the mother he sings about, and I'll understand better.

Slim keeps to himself, but Willie is always happy to chat, to listen to me play guitar and to offer some pointers. During much of their two-week engagement, I make my way to The Ballad Room after school and talk with Willie. I learn his song "Built for Comfort," even though I'm skinny and don't look the part.

A few weeks later, I dare to find myself on The Ballad Room's stage, doing my best Pete Seeger imitation. At age fourteen, I have acquired a longneck banjo, à la Pete, and strive to adopt his vocal characteristics and posture, particularly the way he distinctively slants his head. (Later, after Earl Scruggs comes to town, I trade that banjo for Bernie Krause's Gibson Mastertone, complete with a resonator to make it louder. The longneck will serve Bernie well as he assumes Pete's old chair in the reformed Weavers; the Mastertone will help me chase the rolling three-finger sound that Scruggs perfected, until I finally give up.)

The MC introduces me to the early audience, a scattered group deep into their cocktails and conversations. I delve into Pete's repertoire of labor songs and Woody Guthrie ballads. As when I accompanied Rolf Cahn, I'm on a real stage with lights and a microphone. This stage even has a carpet. But this time I'm accompanying nobody but myself. A bright spotlight hits me head on. On either side of its arc, only darkness where, moments ago, there were chairs and tables and people. Wisps of cigarette smoke waft through the spotlight's path, softening its stark stare and lending a dreamlike, otherworldly cast to the moment. It's a heady experience in several senses: making music, performing, and yes, the applause.

But after its successful opening The Ballad Room runs into problems. It serves alcohol that young people can't buy, and they – unlike the jazz aficionados upstairs at Storyville – are folk music's main audience. It's a paradox: folk music – which is, almost by definition, pretty old – is becoming the sound track of the young. George Wein will later confide, "We didn't lose much money, and we didn't make any money. We did a lot of things like that, in those days."

One morning I find Ramblin' Jack Elliott asleep on the living room couch. His gig at The Ballad Room doesn't begin until the next night, but Manny, aware of Jack's casual attitude towards time – at his last Boston appearance he showed up at eleven for an eight PM concert – has prevailed upon him to arrive a day early.

Jack has rambled in from Britain, where he spent several years as expat folksinger in residence. Although less overtly political than Pete Seeger, he too has deep ties to Woody Guthrie and to the idea of folk music as part of a grassroots movement. He sleeps through the day, and at supper declines Mom's pot roast, as he doesn't like to eat before singing. He begins a long story that continues through the meal, through the car ride, and through his performance. As he bids good-bye, and the story has yet to reach a conclusion, I am forming an alternate notion of his rambling, one that has little to do with geography.

When I first hear Bob Dylan a few years later, at the Indian Neck Folk Festival in Connecticut, he will strike me as imitating Jack Elliott imitating Woody Guthrie. He doesn't adopt Jack's cowboy persona, but has some of his mannerisms. His stories too seem to wander, but he is developing a sense of when to cut them short with a biting phrase that undercuts the setup and turns the tale into a parable that makes you think.

Dear Bob Dylan,

Is "Ramona" a metaphor for your songwriting? The thought came to me the other night, after your concert at Jordan Hall, which my dad presented. But I was mostly struck by a moment in the dressing room, as you were preparing to perform. My mom stopped in briefly, said a few words, inspected the scene, and then left. You sneered and called her "some old chick," and I found myself stuck, paralyzed. Part of me wanted to defend my mother, family honor and all that. Another part of me wanted to stay part of the scene and within your aura. I guess that's the part that won out, because I said nothing. Later the four of us — you, Joan Baez, Eric von Schmidt and me — hunkered down in the van, so you and Joan could stay out of sight of the fans, who were shouting and banging on the doors. That surprised and frightened me. You were used to it.

My "Dear Bob" letter

Manny and Bob

When I next hear him, a few months later at a Boston or Cambridge coffee house, Dylan now sounds like he's directly channeling Guthrie, and no longer needs Elliott as an intermediary.

And a few months later – when he is singing an array of new songs to an impromptu springtime gathering, including Joan Baez, on the sunny banks of the Charles River – he sounds like Bob Dylan, no one else, already confidently poised on the precipice between diffidence and intensity. That boy moves fast.

*4 Huntoon Street then...*

Other house guests visit 4 Huntoon Street: John Jacob Niles, who subverts his patrician bearing by assuming the role of a southern waiter, napkin over his forearm; Oscar Brand, promoting his long-running radio program; and Guy Carawan, fresh from a politically bold trip to China, who takes time to teach me the basics of finger picking – keep that thumb going back and forth, on the beat, while the index and middle fingers either pinch in time with the thumb, or else pluck exactly in between two thumb strokes, in syncopation. Guy suggests that I listen to Merle Travis, master of the style.

Odetta graciously asks how I react to her performance, what songs I respond to. She teaches me how to take a B7 fingering all the way up to the guitar's seventh fret, where, aided by the open sixth string (low E) and the open second string (B), it magically becomes an E7 chord. I can even take a couple of beats to slide it up there, so that the transformation becomes a small journey.

After I grow up and no longer live on Huntoon Street, I continue to see Odetta at intervals. The last time is at the Newport Folk Festival, where I am accompanying Rosalie Sorrels on the same stage, just before Odetta's set. She takes the stage slowly and clearly with some effort. Frail now, and much smaller, she no longer plays guitar and her voice has lost a good deal of its signature resonance. But on this day, she digs deep and draws out a powerful set, crucially informed by the blues. A lesson in tenacity, perseverance and growth.

4 Huntoon Street is my home until I enter college, when my growing up takes on markedly different characteristics.

Geographically it's not a big change. Harvard is a direct subway ride from Dorchester Lower Mills, one that can be navigated in under an hour. But climbing the stairs to Harvard Square means

*Odetta's E7 chord*

entering a different world. People drink espresso here. They walk the streets with serious-looking books under their arms, including poetry that they actually read and understand, and history that goes beyond generals and their battles. Many Cantabrigians sport the marks of prep school, like rep ties and leather patches on the elbows of their tweed jackets. Occasionally you'll see somebody famous, like Nathan Pusey or Henry Kissinger. (John F. Kennedy serves on Harvard's board, but does not come to Cambridge for meetings. His day job gives him the rare power to move the sessions to Washington.)

I have been making this subway trek for a number of years, starting with Joan Baez's and Eric von Schmidt's performances at Club 47. And by 1961, I am performing at the 47 myself, both as soloist, and as accompanist for Jackie Washington, and less formally with others.

But having a room in Harvard Yard – Thayer Hall, where Kennedy spent his freshman year – makes a huge difference. Now I never have to go home; or when I do, it is just down the block, with no worries that the subway may have stopped running, or that my parents will smell my breath.

That room is the first of many homes away from Dorchester Lower Mills. But in 1974, while I'm living in California with Carol, soon to become my second wife, I'll decide to return to Huntoon Street. Carol has been accepted at New England Conservatory of Music, and rather than split up with her, I want to join her new life in Boston. My parents no longer live there – Leona is working for a publisher in Philadelphia, while Manny is establishing Folklore Productions' outpost in Santa Monica – and the house is available. So Carol and I pile our worldly belongings, including several guitars, into my Dodge van and drive east, playing a few gigs along the way.

It takes a while to reacclimate. Huntoon Street seems much the same, but Boston seems to move at a quicker pace and its pop-

*... and more recently*

ulation more varied, less reliably Irish and Italian. Eventually Carol settles into a routine of study combined with waitressing, and I land a series of gigs playing with rhythm-and-blues bands in Roxbury, halfway between Huntoon Street and Boston Latin School.

Houseguests again appear. Some of these are my new bandmates, perhaps the first dark-skinned people on Huntoon Street since Folklore Productions left. And some, like Dave Van Ronk, Rosalie Sorrels and Geoff Muldaur, are refugees from that golden age when folk music was hip.

I've been running into Dave Van Ronk for years, ever since my teenage forays into Greenwich Village, where he presides over the local music scene like a kindly and enlightened lord. Dave's default curmudgeon mode masks a softer side, which he gradually reveals as we get to know each other on the Village's narrow streets and intense music scene. Occasionally I am his houseguest, sleeping on his couch and playing on his album *Songs for Aging Children*.

But in 1976, when he comes to perform at Passim, Club 47's successor, I am the host and he is my houseguest at 4 Huntoon Street. Our friendship deepens. We follow the fortunes of our respective baseball teams, his Mets and my Red Sox. We argue about music – bebop versus trad jazz, and does Alice Coltrane possess anything like her late husband's mojo, and how much swing can a guitar fingerpick? The night grows late, the bottle grows empty, and laughter bounces off the walls of my childhood home.

Not long after Van Ronk leaves, a more sober visit – I receive the startling news that my parents have decided to make their separation legal and binding. And I, as the sole remaining family member in residence, find myself something between a referee and a counselor, as the two of them move from room to room, dividing up the objects that they have accumulated over the decades. At one point, my mom draws me aside to lament that she made two life commitments over the years: one to a man, the other to a political movement. And neither has lasted.

Leona claims the couch that folds into a double bed, where Sonny Terry and so many others have slept. At this point, no one

*Manny and Leona, young and in love*

is laughing at Sonny's song about the key that no longer fits a lock. The couch goes first to Cape Cod, where Leona goes to lick her fresh wounds, and then back to Boston, to her new apartment on Charles Street, Beacon Hill. I will sleep there when I visit. Manny takes his stash, including most of the vinyl recordings, to California, where he establishes a new life. And I wind up with the leftovers, including a bookcase that still does useful work in my guest bedroom in Santa Monica.

In time, my parents will reconnect with much of what brought them together. They take trips to Italy and Spain, and visit with "Uncle" Steve Gardner and other comrades from their younger days. Though no longer the starry-eyed couple who met at that May Day protest march in 1941, standing shoulder to shoulder against fascism, no longer working to keep a young family together, and no longer figuring how to start and keep afloat a business quirkily dedicated to traditional music, they value each other and their shared history.

Not too long after they divide the contents of 4 Huntoon Street, I decide to join my dad in the family business. Carol and I move to Santa Monica, and the house moves into other hands and into other family narratives. I like to think that the music and stories that filled its rooms still hover over its current inhabitants, perhaps leaving a sense of a fleeting moment that seems special, not only to my coming of age, but also to the culture writ large. But even so, I expect that today Huntoon Street is a less musical block than it was back then, when it bore witness to my fitful coming of age.

> *The trolley track still waits at the foot of the hill*
> *And condos fill the shell of that old chocolate mill*
> *And often I ponder as a wanderer does*
> *How I would go home, if I knew where it was*
> *Searching for him still, the boy by the chocolate mill*
>               *–Mitch Greenhill*

## 14 YEARS OLD

*Saturday Night and Sunday Morning with
Reverend Gary Davis*

"Miz Greenhill!" the Reverend rasps, his voice cutting through the chilly Dorchester morning. Grey stubble on his chocolate skin contrasts with the jacket and tie that he wears even to breakfast. One gnarled hand grasps a cup, the other his white cane.

Then he softens, and continues in a mock pleading tone, "Would you please *sanctify* my coffee?" If he weren't blind, you would swear that he winks as he growls, "sanctify."

"Why certainly, Reverend," replies my mother, knowing her part. And she gently pours a shot of whiskey into her guest's cup.

That ongoing dialogue, a secular call-and-response, sits at some remove, but not entirely divorced, from how I imagine Reverend Davis in the pulpit, interacting with the congregation.

Reverend Davis can employ a number of indirect tactics to realize his objectives. One afternoon, the phone rings. My father answers and I hear him talking to the proprietor of Wurlitzer Music, downtown on Boylston Street. It seems that Reverend Davis has taken a fancy to a Gibson J-200 guitar, one of the classiest flattops available, and will not let it out of his grasp. He sits in the center of the store, playing the guitar, caressing it, talking to it. The propri-

*Reverend Davis and Miss Gibson*

etor says that he is upsetting the customers. He is certainly upsetting the proprietor.

"He says to call you, that you're good for it," says the proprietor.

My dad says okay, authorizing the $500 purchase. And so Reverend Davis and "Miss Gibson" begin a long and fruitful relationship. A couple of hours later he brings it home, and my eyes grow wide; it is the biggest and shiniest guitar I have ever seen, maybe twice as big as my father's little nylon job. As to the cash that my father has advanced, "Better I owe you money than you owe me money," Davis says, again with that implied wink. And that is part of the deal.

For me, the payback is plentiful. Reverend Davis, having over the years developed a blind man's need to keep his possessions in hand, does not let Miss Gibson slip from his grip. He sits on our living room couch and plays for hours. When I ask, he breaks down his technique, as fully as any academic I will encounter a few miles north, at Harvard College.

I am in my early teens by now, and starting to get interested in girls. Reverend Davis should be just the right adviser for worldly matters. One day I have a date to meet Sandy Rosenthal downtown. We are both taking classes at Boston Children's Theater and, truth be told, have engaged in a little necking and petting at parties.

But when Gary Davis begins to play, I find it hard to leave. I know that I have made a commitment to be elsewhere. But then Davis starts singing and playing "Samson and Delilah" or "Crucifixion" or even (if Mrs. Davis isn't with him) secular songs like "Candy Man" or "Cocaine Blues" or even...

> *Baby let me lay it on you*
> *Baby let me lay it on you*
> *I'll give you everything in the God almighty world*
> *If you just let me lay it on you*

I guess I lose track of the time. Eventually Sandy calls to ask where I am and what about our date? I'm trying to answer her, but at the same time, Davis is playing some amazing guitar and his gravelly voice fills the household.

Sandy is not amused. "Would you please turn down the radio and tell me what's going on?" she yells, trying to be heard over the music.

"But that's just it," I stammer. "It's not the radio. It's him. He's playing here and now!"

It's not the last time that I wish I could be in two places at once. I want to keep my date with Sandy. Occasionally I make vague moves in that direction, looking for my keys, once even putting on my jacket. My adolescent hormones are telling me to go – it was only last weekend, in the back seat of Charlsie Atwell's Ford, that I got to second base with her; maybe this time I can get farther. But Reverend Davis's holy blues will not let me loose.

I never get to that appointment and never get to lay much of anything on Sandy Rosenthal. Torn and embarrassed, I take off my jacket and resume what now clearly seems to be my necessary position, as a member of Reverend Davis's amen choir. In my own struggle, a metaphorical Sunday morning has won out over Saturday night. My eyes are fixed on the Reverend's meaty hands as they tame, cajole and stimulate that big guitar. The door that Pete Seeger showed me – perhaps this is where I walk through it and choose the musical world on the other side. But now that world seems a bit more complex and intricate. Its hairpin turns need to be navigated with subtle skills that I do not yet possess. I must become a better student, more focused, more dedicated.

*Reverend Davis's C7 chord*

Reverend Davis's unique style derives, as he testifies, "from my own origination." Both hands attack the strings. The thumb and index finger of his right hand often move up and down along one string, like a flatpick. He uses the thumb of his left hand to fret not only the bottom string, but at times the bottom *two* strings – so his version of a C7 chord has the thumb on the third fret of both the fifth and sixth strings, his middle finger on the second fret of the fourth string, his ring finger on the third fret of the third string, his index finger on the first fret of the second string, and his pinky on the third fret of the first string. I've never seen or heard anything like it – he is covering all six strings without a barre, without a capo and without leaving any string open.

The Reverend is a good teacher. His blindness does not prevent him from discerning whether I am playing the note E on my open first string, or on my second string at the fifth fret, or on my third string on the ninth fret. (And how does that relate to the "tonal improvisation" concept being preached by that other Davis – Miles?)

A couple of years later, I take a formal lesson from him, at his second-floor apartment in New York City's northern reaches. An elevated train occasionally screeches past the window, and we pause until it passes.

As the train's metallic clatter recedes, we resume. Reverend Davis is showing me the unique fingerpicking pattern that he employs on "Candy Man," one of his signature pieces. In a sense, it reverses Travis picking, in that Davis's thumb starts

*Reverend Gary Davis, Annie Davis*

on the higher bass string, then the lower. (Travis always moves low to high.) But then the Reverend shows me a four-note bass run that offers an escape route, a way to the more traditional pattern,

*Rev Davis with cigar and 12-string guitar*

low to high. It's kind of like patting your head and rubbing your belly at the same time. The lyrics seem vaguely ribald, at least as far as I can understand them. I get a kick out of the line that he sings in falsetto, "Run and get the bucket, bring the baby some beer."

"How come you use only two fingers to play it?" I ask. I was earlier taught to use three fingers, Travis-style.

"Because that's all you need."

Mrs. Davis busies herself in the next room. She is more religiously observant than the Reverend, who moves at will between his own worlds of Saturday night and Sunday morning, at least when she's not around. In her presence, he invokes the gospels – including the Armageddon-tinged Book of Revelations in "Twelve Gates To the City." He is sure that he will meet his mother in Galilee.

But back in Boston, on the road as a traveling musician, he likes a good party, a stiff drink, and a pretty girl. He often sidles up to some wan Radcliffe student. He'll put his hand on her knee, as he attempts to get to know her better. Here his blindness is helpful: what he can't see, he must feel. Many years later I ask one such beauty if the Reverend ever scored with one of these ladies. "Oh no, I don't think so," she recalls, with a secret smile.

Reverend Davis's lessons include paradoxes and contradictions. The worlds of the spirit and the flesh comprise two distinct but related keys

*Reverend Davis in repose*

within a musical passage. Eventually it is the secular key that unlocks the door to financial success, as his songs are discovered and recorded by the likes of the Rolling Stones, Jackson Browne, and Bob Dylan, who calls Davis "one of the wizards of modern music." The proceeds flow first to my dad's company, then on to Reverend and Mrs. Davis, who purchase a brick house in Queens, the first and only home that they own. Mrs. Davis manages to overlook any contradictions in accepting profit from such questionable sources.

In my later teenage years, my father and I visit them there. Manny needs to go over some business with Reverend Davis, perhaps a recording contract, perhaps the matter of that $500 loan for Miss Gibson, which remains outstanding. I want to check in with Miss Gibson and pick up some new musical pointers.

We find Davis a good deal heavier. He has begun to eat well and often, his expanding belly a testament to his art, his business acumen, and his perseverance. The business concluded, we are offered some light refreshment. The good Reverend sits back and fires up a cigar, draws deeply on it, and then exhales. The smoke curls first around a lace lampshade, then up to the ceiling of his very own living room. It's a long way from the Carolina streets where, as Blind Gary, he first began to sing for a living. Those secular songs, blues and party tunes, were his first meal ticket, before religion opened another door to a different passageway. And now, as neatly as any leftist college student in his Ivy League audience, he has synthesized the dialectic.

It's a lesson in the winding road that music can send one on. The lesson of Saturday night and Sunday morning. And a lesson in the power of conviction and commitment as tools for navigating the path's curves and contradictions. Whenever I encounter Reverend Davis, he presents himself confidently as a powerful agent of art; I never see him nervous or unsettled. On more than one occasion, I even see him fall asleep on stage.

The next day, I'm back in my bedroom, hunkered over my Gibson J-45, still trying to decode "Candy Man."

> *Candy Man, been here and gone*
> *Candy Man, been here and gone*
> *Candy Man, been here and gone*
> *I'd give anything in this God almighty world,*
> *to get my Candy Man home*
> — *Reverend Gary Davis*

# 15 YEARS OLD
## The Artist's Life with Eric von Schmidt

At a concert presented by the Folk Song Society of Greater Boston, Rolf Cahn is joined onstage by Eric von Schmidt, who sings "Grizzly Bear," his one-chord reinterpretation of a chain-gang work song. Rolf has just changed guitar strings, but has not snipped off the looped extra lengths, which dance and jangle above the peghead, as his left hand moves up and down the fretboard. He is in Sister Rosetta Tharpe mode, using double-stops with open strings to create a rich melodic interpretation of this originally a cappella song. Eric sticks with a basic A7 chord throughout, as he growls about the "great big grizzly, grizzly bear."

Where Rolf is precise and cerebral and didactic, Eric is loose and emotional. Where Rolf approaches the blues intellectually, almost as an American cousin of European existentialism, Eric seems to have internalized the music. I feel drawn to him as a different sort of mentor. He has some sort of deep relationship to this emblematic grizzly bear. And when he sings, "Jack of diamonds is a hard card to play," or "Stick with me, baby, I'll turn your money green," I fully believe him, see him at the card table or wherever the song places him.

To sing "Wasn't That a Mighty Storm" – a ferocious ballad about a flood that he learned from a Library of Congress recording

*Mitch, Rolf Cahn, Eric von Schmidt at Club 47*

by the deliciously named Sinkiller Griffin – he tunes the guitar to an open G chord, places it on his lap, and uses a knife to slide up the fretboard with his left hand.

*Wasn't that a mighty storm!*
*Blew all the people all away*

Von Schmidt is a mighty storm unto himself. He blows away a lot of people, including me.

After Rolf leaves Boston for the West Coast, I drift into Eric's orbit and under the spell of his charisma. I regularly attend his one-night-a-week residency at Club 47, near Harvard Square. While the 47 focuses mainly on jazz, featuring local luminaries like Sam Rivers and Tony Williams, it sets aside two nights for newly popular "folk music." In addition to Eric, the other non-jazz regular is a shy teenage soprano named Joan Baez.

The more I learn about Eric von Schmidt's talents – in addition to music, he is a trained painter and illustrator, has lived in Europe and on tropical islands, cooks a mean *crêpe*, and is working on a couple of films – the more I want to be close to him. Eric is receptive, and at one point invites me to stop by after school, to visit the Cambridge apartment where he lives with his wife and their baby daughter.

By now I am a high school sophomore at Boston Latin School. The venerable institution has, by the 1950s, somewhat lost its luster. I don't much like the place, find it stuffy, stodgy and old-fashioned, a bastion of hierarchical rote learning.

Of Boston Latin's many quirks, one of the most salient is compulsory ROTC – Reserve Officers Training Corps. Several times a week, we teenagers, dressed in army khakis, hoist dummy rifles on our shoulders and march in formation around the tarmac that passes for a school playground. I guess we are getting ready to fend off the imminent Soviet invasion they are always telling us about.

It is on one such day that I arrive at Eric's Cambridge apartment. I am still wearing my ROTC uniform, with Latin School's purple-and-gold insignia patched onto my khaki shoulder, as I make my way past Cambridge landmarks that are fast becoming part of my own visual vocabulary: Cahaly's Market and Tommy's Lunch on Mount Auburn Street, both next to Club 47, and the Hayes-Bickford Cafeteria, which sells coffee brewed last week, and where Joan Baez was once asked to leave because she dared to start singing.

In the apartment, spools of 16-millimeter film unfurl in curlicues from where Eric has tacked them on the wall, barely out of reach from his one-year-old toddler. He is nursing a rum-and-tonic (Bacardi dark) as he works on this film, a dramatization of a traditional ballad, "The Young Man Who Wouldn't Hoe Corn."

Up close, concentrating on the spools of film, he at

*Eric, Mitch, Maria Muldaur at the Newport Folk Festival*

first seems more sinewy and smaller than on stage, where, big and bearded, his presence seems to fill the room. But when he sees my uniform, he turns his full attention to me, and it is I who feel very small. Eric is horrified. To him, I am dressed in a symbol of imperial militarism, perpetuating the Cold War and perhaps leading us to nuclear Armageddon. "Get. Out. Of. Here," he orders. He seems like that grizzly bear, disturbed in his lair, growling to protect his offspring – the film, as well as the baby – from a predator. He won't have the uniform – or me – in his creative home. I am banished.

Mortified and humiliated, I slink away. I find the uniform silly and resent the rule that makes me wear it. But hadn't thought that I was complicit in war crimes. I stumble to the subway and make my humble way back to Dorchester, where military uniforms are tolerated, even admired.

But, as Eric later points out, "You came back." That, to him, is the important thing. I come back for the juice, the energy, the creative oomph that Eric carries with him at all times. After a few visits, I finally feel accepted by this big presence. Our relationship develops and deepens.

Four years later, more to receive his imprimatur than because he's my closest friend, I ask Eric to serve as best man at my wedding. He shows up in a white suit and a nasty hangover. The bride is Louise Rice, who will become the mother of my two children. The first, Matthew, is born while I am with Eric in Westport, Connecticut, preparing material for an album that we hope Vanguard Records will record and release. When word of Matthew's arrival comes, I drive back to Cambridge. "It's a boy!" Louise smiles wearily. Later that week I return to Westport, giving cigars to the toll collectors on the Massachusetts Turnpike. But Vanguard rejects the album, and we put it off for another day.

Westport is the family home, legacy of Eric's father, Harold von Schmidt, renowned painter of western themes. Even after the main house is sold, Eric retains the studio until the end of his days. Once I find Paul Newman there, discussing graphics for one of his charitable projects. Newman's eyes are as improbably blue as any publicist might describe.

I continue to follow Eric's journey when he buys a Shaker-built farmhouse near Henniker, New Hampshire. The Shakers did not believe in creature comforts, as is clear when you sit on the straight wooden bench by the stove. But Eric has made the place warm and welcoming.

In the basement, under the influence of peyote, I marvel at the massive granite stones that form the foundation. A few centuries ago, teams of oxen must have hauled them from a regional quarry. Singer Geoff Muldaur and Richard Fariña, Eric's writer and musician friend, join me in chanting, our voices echoing off the stones and surrounding us with a blanket of sound.

By now I've surrendered to the peyote. The big stones are pulsing and showing an array of colors that had previously lain hidden. The candlelight too seems alive. I feel close to Geoff and Eric, my good friends. And Richard too now seems a kindred spirit. It was only a few weeks ago that he and his new bride, the former Mimi Baez, returned from Spain for their initial performance at Club 47. I was the opening act. Richard is suave, perhaps a bit too smooth for our rough-hewn crowd. But he's so damn nice that I feel myself warming to him.

And suddenly I'm missing Louise. She's back in Cambridge, but I want her here with me, right now. Geoff half-heartedly encourages me when I decide to phone her and prevail upon her better sense. But Richard is sympathetic to Louise when she resists my peyote-fueled phone plea to drive north in the dark and join us, keep me company. Richard is empathetic, good at seeing other points of view. This gift stands him in good stead as he works on his novel, *Been Down So Long It Looks Like Up To Me*, which he finishes after leaving Cambridge for California. It is a seemingly wild, even over-the-top tale of college rebellion. But it doesn't seem too odd a few years later, when Harvard and other colleges will be shut down by students against the war in Vietnam.

In that, Richard is prescient. But his own fate takes him, and all of us, by surprise. On the day the book is published, snugly blanketed under Eric's cover painting, he is killed in a motorcycle accident on the Big Sur coast.

When Betsy Siggins calls with news of Richard's death, it becomes my task to inform Eric. I reach him in Florida, where he is spending the winter. At first he is happy to hear from me, and launches into a jokey anecdote. When I interrupt with the tragic news, he is thrown off stride, asks a few questions, then becomes quiet and rings off.

The next day he calls back. He thanks me for the call and apologizes for being so abrupt. "Last night I heard a strange noise," he says. "Coming from outside my bedroom. It was a knocking sound, distant but close, too." He voices a painful chuckle. "I was

*Accompanying my mentor, with a careful eye on his chord hand*

*Eric, Geoff Muldaur, Jenny Muldaur, Mitch at Newport Folk Festival, 1980s*

sure it was Richard, saying goodbye." It would be just like Richard, who always loved magic and mystery, to exit with such a flourish. We decide to ignore the logical explanation that eventually surfaces – a dangling board that the wind pushes into the siding – and give Richard his final credit as trickster.

In the winter of 1966 Louise and I visit Eric in Florida. He is the host of creative fun, as well as of creative work, leading leisurely games of bocce ball on the beach. He cooks a feast to commemorate something he calls East Prussian Combination Pride and Shame Day.

One wall of his painting studio is dominated by large canvases, vast smoky epics of nineteenth-century American life. Paintbrush and palette in hand, he has to climb a ladder to work on the upper regions. There he squeezes paint from a tube, mixes it with another color, and touches up a mysterious corner. On the opposite wall, he is working on illustrations for *The Joan Baez Songbook*, each song rendered in delicate collage. Clothing is indicated by scraps of pattern pasted on to painted backdrops, and faces are hand-drawn in pen-and-ink. His motor seems perpetually on. Even his letters and cards are masterpieces of intricate and expressive calligraphy, some of it backwards mirror-style and full of inside jokes..

After I have followed Eric to a number of places, Eric follows me to California, where I finally convince Mercury Records to record the album that Vanguard shelved. It's now 1968 and, at age 24, I assume the role of album producer. The result is *Who Knocked the Brains Out Of the Sky*, to be released later that year. Eric has created an array of characters in these original songs, including "Lucky Mrs. Ticklefeather" and "Weep For the Wooden Man," a riff on his Teutonic heritage. I'm writing cello lines, and learning about drum sounds, and finding musicians who can play hurdy-gurdy and calliope. Not to mention navigating the new need first to create a budget, and then to meet it. And as I'm making my share of rookie mistakes (some of those tempos!), I'm also beginning to free-fall down the rabbit hole of studio life, where hours, days and weeks slip by stealthily, while one's ears are otherwise occupied. That's a magnetic pull that will only grow stronger in the years to come.

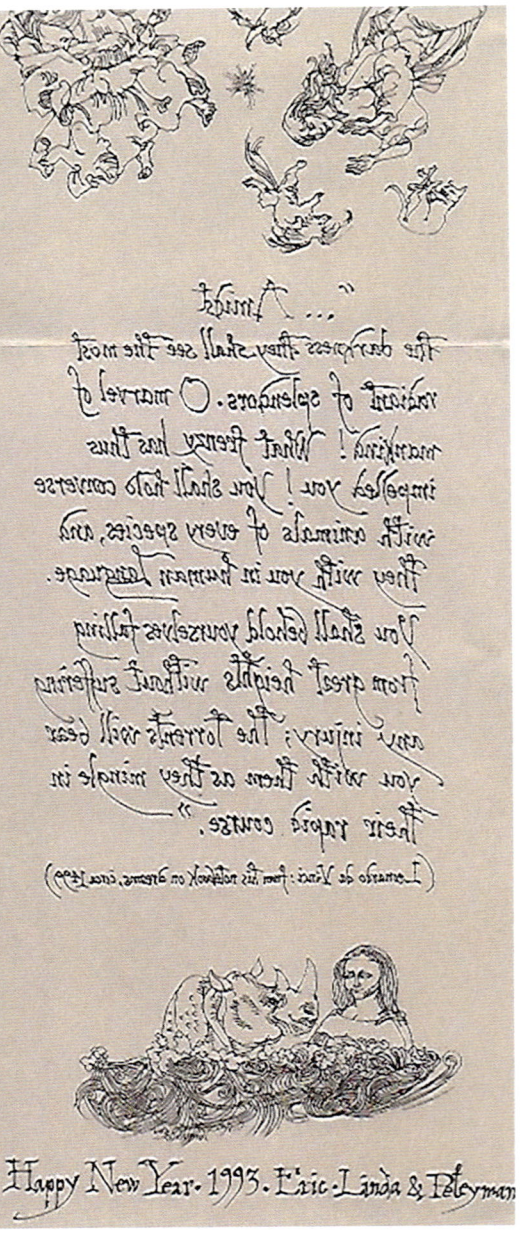

*New Year's greeting from Eric von Schmidt*

Bob Dylan writes in the liner notes that Eric "can separate the men from the boys and the note from the noise; the bridle from the saddle and the cow from the cattle. He can play the tune of the moon, the why of the sky, and the commotion of the ocean. Yes he can – and he also is a hell of a guy."

Eric's recording intrigues another cultural maverick. "He seems like one of the few originals still floating around," writes Hunter Thompson.

As the years pass and we live on opposite sides of the continent, Eric and I see each other less frequently. When we do connect, I notice that his angry side has grown more dominant. Maybe he becomes jealous of the mainstream success that eludes him while it blesses Dylan and Baez. Maybe it is the accumulated rum-and-tonics. But for whatever reason, the chip on Eric's shoulder grows as he ages. He picks a fight with one friend over their divergent theories on American Indian war practices, and questions another's decision to join Alcoholics Anonymous.

The last time I see him, it does not go well. It's 2002, and I have a gig working as sound designer and composer at Trinity Repertory Theatre in Providence. The production is August Wilson's *The Piano Lesson*, a powerful piece that speaks to me in a couple of ways: it welcomes my knowledge of African-American music; and it poses questions about one's legacy, how to handle one's birthright.

I decide to spend my day off by driving south to Westport, where Eric, who provided such crucial guidance when I first ventured into the world of African-American music, has returned to live. The big house of his childhood has been sold; the old painting studio is now his home. That's his legacy; mine is Folklore Productions.

It will be our first visit in several years, and the first since he lost his vocal cords to throat cancer. Eric and I communicate by fax – although, as it turns out, not very well – and I rent a car. Several hours later, as snow begins to fall, I turn into his driveway, then knock on his door. No answer, but the door is unlocked and the snow is growing heavier, so I let myself in and admire a couple of new paintings on the wall.

Eric, when he arrives, is not happy to see me. He is recovering from a sudden hernia operation and wants to be left alone. In lieu of a voice, he communicates through a mechanical box in his throat. He is clearly frustrated at having to press this button on his throat to activate the tool that gives him only minimal command of language. "Read. The. Damn. Fax," he croaks in a robotic voice far removed from his own. But the message is clear, and I am soon out in the snow. This time, unlike when my teenage military garb led to banishment, I do not come back.

The ride back to Providence, through what is now a major storm, is ugly and a bit dangerous. I join a long line of cars and semi-tandems slowly snaking north on the Connecticut Turnpike. My wipers work to sweep the precipitation from blocking my windshield, but it's hard to see more than a few feet ahead, where the parade of vehicles inches through wet piles of snow and slush. On an uphill grade in southern Rhode Island, I lose control and find myself swerving into almost a full right turn. But then, somehow, the car regains traction, and makes it up and over the hill.

Eventually I reach Providence, where I return the rented vehicle and find safe harbor in my hotel's bar. The hotel finally delivers Eric's last fax, telling me not to come.

Beset by a slew of physical ailments, Eric dies a couple of years later.

From Eric I learn to see art as life and vice versa. To him art is not distinct from life; they are one and the same.

In the late 1980's, when my wanderlust leads me to spend my midlife crisis as an international traveler, I will recognize this in Bali, where art is everywhere. In the morning, women make intricate miniature flower arrangements, then place them along the road, where the afternoon rains wash them away.

As I watch the blossoms float down towards the sea, I think of Eric, who strives, I think, for a more permanent artistic legacy. The creative impulse is the same – a vision of fleeting beauty may be all we can expect. Still, Eric was a work of art unto himself – complex, challenging, beautiful, and eventually swept away.

*Weep for the wooden man*
*Remember if you can*
*Remember a time when he did stand.*
– Eric von Schmidt

*Caitlin von Schmidt and father*

## 15 YEARS OLD
*Divided Loyalties with Merle Travis*

I knock on the door with some trepidation. For one thing, hotels are unfamiliar to me, even hotels in Boston. For another, I am about to meet Merle Travis, an idol since my first attempts, not that long ago, at learning to fingerpick the guitar. Or, as we call it, Travis picking, keeping a steady bass line with the thumb, while the fingers pluck the melody on the higher strings. The Rosetta Stone of this mystery is a recording called *Folk Songs of the Hills*, which Travis initially released as a children's album, its traditional and original songs and stories of cute animals strewn casually over a magical vocabulary of guitar lore. Initial stabs at deciphering it have suggested vast musical vistas in the world beyond.

Noises come from behind the door, perhaps the creak of bedsprings, the shuffle of slippered feet, the rustle of clothing. Then the door opens and here he is, smaller than I had imagined. I am surprised to find him in pajamas and robe, and wonder if my father has told him to expect me.

*Merle Travis*

## 15 YEARS OLD: DIVIDED LOYALTIES WITH MERLE TRAVIS

I am fresh from sixth period at Boston Latin School, a few blocks away. Around the corner stands Jordan Hall, high temple of chamber music, where Travis is scheduled to perform a few hours later. The presenter is Folklore Productions, which has grown into a regular presenter of concerts, and a manager and booker of artists. The company now presents a dozen or so concerts each season, and the artist roster includes Joan Baez. The young company is feeding a growing hunger, especially among the city's large student population, for the substantial fare of folk music, in the term's broader sense. The Merle Travis concert features a guitar virtuoso, so should appeal to the growing army of pickers that is becoming a substantial presence on each of the area's many campuses.

I'm not sure whether my dad fully believes rumors that Travis may be too friendly with the bottle, or if he just wants to channel my hero-worship into a useful direction. Whatever the reason, I have been dispatched as Folklore Productions' emissary, assigned to keep the guitar legend company. And to deliver him sober before showtime.

Invited in, I nervously stumble across the threshold, and am soon face-to-face with Merle Travis. He too seems nervous, but possesses the skill of Southern manners, which he uses to put both of us, if not at ease, at least in the middle of a conversation. He is courteous and even a bit courtly, ready to make me welcome and willing to respond to questions. Not yet aware of his years as a major country-and-western star, with rhinestones on his clothes and elaborate mother-of-pearl on his guitar neck, I ask about hard times in Kentucky, about the lives of coal miners so tellingly evoked in his great songs "Dark as a Dungeon" and "Sixteen Tons." He responds with questions of his own, perhaps already getting a bead on the audience that awaits him, a crowd more used to Pete Seeger's work shirts than to sharp costuming from flashy haberdashers like Nudie's Rodeo Tailors.

When he suggests that we share a few beers, I find myself in a deep moral dilemma. Do my loyalties lie with family, sobriety and the upcoming concert? Or with my new friend and long-time hero, who is even now rendering my doubts irrelevant as he negotiates on the phone with room service (*room service!*) for a couple of six-packs?

As in Travis picking, even the most carefully mapped passages can at times be navigated only with the aid of improvisation. "Sure," I improvise.

After the phone call and an awkward wait, there is a knock on the door, and the dangerous beverages arrive, courtesy of an elderly, ramrod-straight gentleman wearing a red tuxedo. With a flourish, he unfurls a white napkin, carefully places the bottles on a table, accepts a gratuity, and is gone. Merle Travis and I are again alone, except for the new alcoholic presence that now seems to dominate the room. My host makes quick use of a bottle opener, pours a couple of glasses, and resumes conversing, now with a bit more energy. I'm trying to hold my own in that department, partly to justify my place in a suddenly adult world, and partly to keep him from overindulging. Did he just now start to drink a second beer, or maybe a third? I'm still on my first, I think. The conversation has veered from the dark hills of Kentucky, of which I know little, to the bright lights of Nashville, of which I know even less. Are there coal miners in Nashville? Or is that where singers sing about hard times that they have no desire to relive?

My thoughts turn to Jordan Hall, where I imagine the crew is just now arriving, in preparation for the evening concert. What sort of shape will Travis be in, I wonder? Will the audience be angry? Will my dad? I start another beer. Tastes pretty good, and it's too late now. May as well enjoy the ride.

The rest of the afternoon passes comfortably, or so I later surmise. Travis untaps a font of anecdotes that continue through the darkening hours. That night he plays brilliantly, gently bank-

# 15 YEARS OLD: DIVIDED LOYALTIES WITH MERLE TRAVIS

ing rich caroms of acoustic guitar tone off Jordan Hall's hallowed walls, and is in total command of both his faculties and his audience. I, on the other hand, wobble a bit and go to bed with a bad headache. At school the next morning my Latin grammar lacks the precision of Travis's bass lines. Dative and ablative cases commingle inappropriately, and at least one verb refuses to budge from the confunktive mood. But in my mind I can hear and see Travis picking with new clarity, and that helps me get through the day, and ultimately through high school. Later that afternoon I pick up my guitar and try my best to make it sound like Merle's – clean, dynamic and clearly conjugating the present tense. My fingers still have a long way to travel, but my mind has a better grasp of the goal.

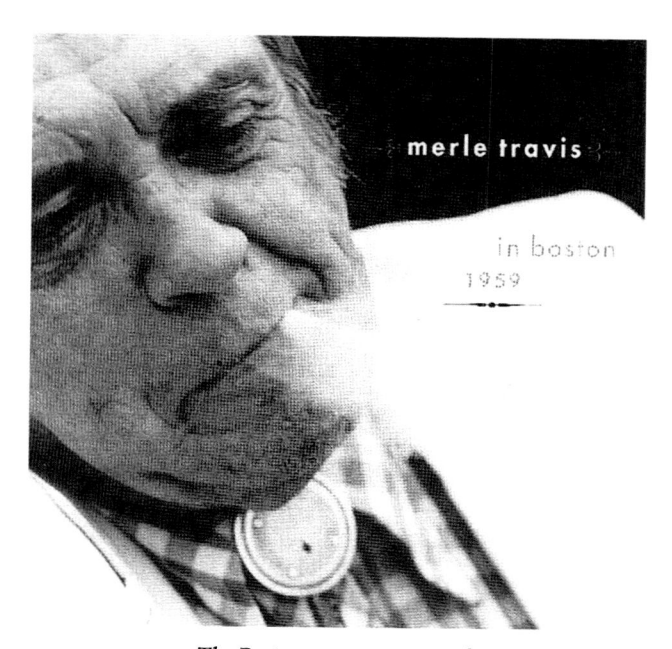

*The Boston concert, preserved*

# 16 YEARS OLD
*Breaking Boundaries with Lightnin' Hopkins*

Sam "Lightnin'" Hopkins is a problematic houseguest. Where others praise my mother's pot roast and, with less justification, the comfort of our guest bed, a lumpy convertible sofa, Lightnin' is having none of that. On the first morning, he finds the scrambled eggs too runny, an opinion he expresses by spitting them onto the kitchen wall. To my mother this is a serious transgression, and I can see her inner struggle between, on the one hand, standing up for herself and, on the other, placating an honored guest who is also a musical artist on the roster of the family business. The latter choice prevails, but just barely. To a teenage boy itching to challenge parental restrictions, the egg incident, disrupting the morning sunlit kitchen, is a source of secret glee. Nobody behaves that way with my mother – certainly not me. It looks like this new potential mentor blasts through normal boundaries. Do I dare to follow?

So this is a different kind of presence – transgressive, wild. The night before, as I'm leaving the bathroom and my early attempts at shaving the light fuzz that is beginning to take root on my chin, I encounter Lightnin' striding towards me through the upstairs hallway. He needs the bathroom to work on straightening his hair, now jauntily enwrapped under the first do-rag I have ever encountered.. Lightnin' is a man whose shiny straight black hair and sparkling gold teeth are as much a part of his persona as his opinions about breakfast. He sings about a mojo hand, about a black Cadillac, and about a bald-headed woman.

*Give me back that wig I bought you, let your doggone head go bald*
*Give me back that wig I bought you, let your doggone head go bald*
*I got the news this morning, little girl, you don't need no hair at all.*

*Lightnin' Hopkins*

In the evenings he prefers gin, a lesson that accompanies his guitar demonstrations. He is a man to be followed, if you can keep up.

My eyes grow wide as he shows me secrets of the key of E. His thumb stays home on the sixth string, open E, which he uses as a recurrent pedal drone. Meanwhile, his index and ring fingers are dancing along the tenth and twelfth frets of the first and second strings. "But Lightnin', how will you manage to navigate down to the lower octave for one of your signature descending runs?" I wonder. "Watch me, young man," he grins, his gold tooth twinkling in the morning sunlight. The secret is the open first string – his left hand glides seamlessly from the 3rd string/12th fret G, to the open 1st, E, then continues down the other strings, on the lower frets, all the way down to the open 6th string, low E.

I'm not sure if this would pass muster with either of the Davis tonal watchdogs, Miles or Reverend Gary, but I am thrilled. I have just learned a three-octave run, not to mention a new geography of the fret board. My algebra homework can wait.

But not my driver's test. The automobile and the open road beckon me. They tease my already well-developed wanderlust and skepticism about boundaries. There was that time, as a 4-year-old, when I tried to commandeer the family DeSoto. Later, in my pre-teens, the subway transported me to distant destinations. I liked to ride in the front car and to press my face against the front window, my eyes glued to the tunnel's farthest reaches. Staring into the darkness of the unknown, I would lose myself in the journey. Sometimes I'd pick a destination at random, in the system's outer regions, where I'd never been before. But now I am old enough to realize the freedom of the endless highway. Now maybe my time has come.

My mother drives me to the Department of Motor Vehicles. When the inspector asks her to move to the back seat, she does so in a decidedly neutral manner, without giving me a glance of encouragement. The inspector sits up front, next to me at the wheel, and instructs me to drive. At first, things go smoothly. I start the car and proceed slowly along Blue Hill Avenue, navigating the social contract at a leisurely twenty-five miles per hour. Then I'm instructed to turn onto a narrow side street, and here I encounter a problem. The three-point turn, reversing direction without room for a full U-turn, stumps me at first. I'm having more trouble navigating the three-point turn than navigating Lightnin''s three-octave run. I can't seem to get the car into reverse; the gearshift instead seems intent on staying in forward gear. I sweat and turn red. My mother sits impassively in the back seat, not moving a muscle; the inspector, representing the Commonwealth of Massachusetts, is stoically non-communicative. Is he scornful of my lack of skill, or sympathetic? As with my mother in back, it's impossible to tell. I'll have to figure this one out on my own.

Finally, I get into reverse gear and drive the car back to the DMV office. I am sure that I have flunked. But instead, I learn that I have passed. "I guess you showed that you didn't panic," my mother suggests. And for the first time that day, she gives an encouraging smile.

If I'm going to explore what lies beyond known boundaries, I have now acquired an important tool to do so. My horizons are broader this afternoon than they seemed this morning.

With my new license, I now offer my services as Lightnin''s designated driver, for his series of New England concerts. When both Lightnin' and my parents agree, I'm excited and leap at the chance. After we carefully load the guitar into the trunk, I navigate the family car through Dorchester's familiar streets, then the outer suburbs, and rural Massachusetts. As we reach the Connecticut state line, Lightnin' offers the bottle that he's been nursing. Not willing to jeopardize my new passport into quasi-adulthood, I refuse, and keep my eyes firmly on the road. After several hours, we approach the Gothic Revival towers of Yale University in New Haven. The stately campus, to my eyes, seems to tolerate rather than to welcome us.

The first person we encounter is last year's class president from Boston Latin School, a popular, accomplished and intimidating figure whom I'll call Three Names, in recognition of his patrician bearing. Back then he never paid much attention to a lower-classman like me, and now I wonder if Three Names will even remember me. In the echoing hallways and assembly halls of high school, I more or less got used to his looking right through me, as his eyes sought out schoolmates with more power, influence or cachet. Will I again be ignored?

But no, Three Names now rushes up and vigorously pumps my hand. Delighted to see me, he touts his standing as the number one Yale freshman. It's almost as if he's now trying to impress me, instead of the other way around. The blues and its special emissary have given me the satisfaction of revenge. Feigning nonchalance, I introduce him to the visiting blues scholar from Houston, the true object of his interest. Lightnin', whose nonchalance is not at all feigned, accepts the proffered handshake and, flashing that gold-tooth smile, calls for an inspection of the performance space and dressing room. Three Names eagerly, even obsequiously complies, and soon we are in a carpeted lounge that has been set aside for Dr. Hopkins. Lightnin', equally comfortable here at Yale as in my family's home in Dorchester and, I assume, in Houston's more dangerous Third Ward, sips from his bottle of gin, unpacks his guitar, and plays a couple of his amazing licks.

In the concert, his introductions to the songs are, to my ears, a bit distant and ironic. I'm anticipating the tortured blues artist, full of hard times and misery. But here Lightnin' becomes the crowd-pleasing showman. He's here to entertain, and he takes his time doing so, comfortable in his own skin. But when he gets down to the music, he digs deeply into the blues. I'm learning that these two faces can coexist, like Janus, the Roman god of beginnings and transitions, or perhaps like the comedy and tragedy masks that I encountered at Boston Children's Theater. Lightnin' is correcting my misperceptions yet again.

The Ivy Leaguers give Lightnin' Hopkins a standing ovation, which he graciously acknowledges as his due. He plays an encore or two. I'm basking in the reflected glory of my companion. When Three Names entreats us to please stay for an after-concert party, we politely decline. And then, Yale conquered, we head back to Boston, emptying the rest of the bottle along the way. This time, when Lightnin' offers the bottle, I shrug and accept. As the gin burns my throat, I concentrate more intensely on my driving. The road is starting to seem like home.

*Lightnin' the entertainer*

As we reach the Massachusetts state line, and the last drops of gin, I venture to ask how Lightnin' enjoys performing for northern white audiences. Does he miss his traditional crowd in Houston's rough-and-tumble bars and roadhouses? Does the Ivy League seem a bit foreign and overly sanitized to him?

"Naw," he says, emptying the bottle. "These white folks pay attention and listen." He looks out the window at a subdivision of cookie-cutter houses, and I imagine that his mind is replaying any number of dicey moments back home in Texas. A young deer has emerged from the surrounding woods to explore a small cherry tree in someone's back yard. "Back home they just drink and make noise," he muses. A light snow begins to fall.

During the following years, as I make my way through the end of adolescence, I continue to run into Lightnin' occasionally, at nightclubs, coffeehouses, and concerts. It's always a treat to reconnect with him and receive the full magic of his blues. At the Newport Folk Festival, where he holds sway over an audience of

*Lightnin', Mitch, Chris Strachwitz of Arhoolie Records at the Newport Folk Festival*

thousands, his performance is especially powerful. I think of our quirky history and feel a special bond.

Then, as I grow older – college, family, new friends – our paths diverge. I move west and we lose touch.

I last encounter him in San Francisco, maybe some fifteen years later. I have just finished playing guitar behind Rosalie Sorrels at an upscale nightclub in Ghirardelli Square. Upscale in that it has carpet and tablecloths. I'm a working musician now, fully running with the herd. Rosalie is a singer-songwriter who left her home and marriage in Salt Lake City to strike out on her own, and her story has made her something of an icon to a group of independent-minded women. Tonight they form a solidly supportive audience, a new and different herd. These women – and Rosalie herself – have a tough-yet-tender way that makes me feel at home. Come to think of it – and given some distance from my teenage home life – my mother is that kind of woman.

Maybe it's this familiar sense of belonging that inspires a flirtation with Polly Ann, a dark-haired writer whose serious demeanor is leavened by an occasional secret smile. She approaches first Rosalie and then me, as we are packing up and preparing to leave the club. Newly divorced, I'm ready for romantic adventure. As Rosalie and I ponder our after-hours options, Polly Ann seems eager to join us.

Polly Ann asks if we're interested in catching the late set that Lightnin' Hopkins will soon perform in foggy North Beach, about a mile away, and that seems like the perfect place to unwind. On the ride there, Polly Ann and I find ourselves together in the back seat of Rosalie's Ford Econoline. She laughs at my jokes, and when I venture to put my arm around her shoulder, she snuggles closer. This is starting to seem promising. At the wheel, Rosalie navigates the hilly neighborhood and parks the car. Our little group picks our way past North Beach's topless bars and Italian bistros, and finally we locate the venue. It's a room that has clearly seen better days, is in fact a bit on the seedy side. The floor is kind of sticky and the stage, where Lightnin' is just now seating himself, is dimly lit in a corner. The sparse audience seems about equally divided between tipsy tourists and music lovers who have some idea of the artist's importance.

Lightnin', older and lacking some of the vitality that I remember, moves slowly and is clearly battling some health issues. Fiddling with the microphone and his chair, he takes a while to get started. I'm

*Mitch, Lightnin', Louise at the Newport Folk Festival*

*Lightnin' at work later in life*

starting to get nervous for him – will he be able to pull it off? But when he begins to sing and play, his powerful presence still shines through. He plays the blues just like Lightnin' Hopkins, which means like no one before or since. He is weak, but he still has that magic.

At the end of the set, I make my way to his dressing room. I have to prompt him to recognize me, as my look has changed. My hair is long now, and my new beard is far more substantial than the peach fuzz of my mid-teens, when I had just begun to shave. The Pete Seeger-inspired flannel shirts of those years have morphed into tye-dye and fringe, covered with a wool poncho from South America. And I imagine that I'm carrying myself a bit differently than when I was sixteen.

When Lightnin' does make the connection, he beams that smile, and the gold tooth sparkles once again. "Young man!" he exclaims, offering his hand. Lightnin''s hair is still jet black, perhaps blacker than when that was its natural color. Rather than present-

## 16 YEARS OLD: BREAKING BOUNDARIES WITH LIGHTNIN' HOPKINS   85

*A younger Lightnin' back in Houston*

ing a mask of youth, it serves to emphasize the deep crevasses that traverse his face, like so many miles of hard road. He idly passes his fingers over the guitar, perhaps a ghost of that three-octave run, as we recall my adolescence and his wayward mentorship.

Polly Ann pops her head in, flashes that smile and says that she and Rosalie are moving on to Spec's Bar, a few blocks down the hill. Feeling torn between my hormones and my guitar hero, I tell her I'll be along soon. I have this idea that Lightnin' will join us at Spec's bar, where I can again, as at Yale, bask in the glory of our relationship, without losing the chance of getting close to Polly Ann. But Lightnin' is not interested in another bar and another hangout; he seems more interested in a good night's sleep. Rather than transgressing any boundaries, he seems bent on enforcing the basic working musician's maxim: don't leave until you get paid.

The two of us spend a while longer in the small dressing room, its plaster peeling in North Beach's damp air. The fog seems everywhere, even inside, where it starts to blur Lightnin's reflection in the cracked mirror. In this room I can sense the spirits of musicians past, all of them waiting for a resolution of some kind, like a dominant 7 chord looking for a tonic. A waitress has gone to look for the proprietor and Lightnin''s money. The frisson of our renewed connection dissipates as he waits, still communing casually with his guitar. Eventually I bid him good night, meaning goodbye.

> *Soon my work will all be done*
> *Soon my work will all be done*
> *Soon my work will all be done*
>     *I'm going home…*
>         —Reverend Gary Davis

## 16-20 YEARS OLD
*A Wider World with Jackie Washington*

The Golden Vanity, the same faux-nautical coffeehouse where Eric von Schmidt accompanied Sonny Terry, runs an open microphone night, when anyone can sign up and perform. One day Juán Cándido Washington y Landrón and a couple of his buddies from the Puerto Rican neighborhood decide to check the place out. "I was part of a very bourgeois group of young people in Roxbury, Massachusetts," Jack Landrón will tell me, some decades later, from the advanced perspective of middle age, "And we heard that there were 'coffeehouses,' places where you could go and there were weird types, loose white women, and people with bones through their noses ..."

In 2005 Jack and I are sitting in a restaurant in Greenwich Village. A veteran of half a century on musical and theatrical stages, he speaks comfortably into the tape recorder, with a hint of ironic distance, as he evokes his younger self.

"I was wearing a herringbone green tight three-button Ivy League suit and a button-down broadcloth shirt and a silk rep tie. That's just what we wore when we went out ...

"We walked into that place and nobody was wearing anything like what we had on. They were all sitting around – I can't even remember what they wore, but they all looked wild. They looked dirty.

"We ordered the stuff that they had on the menu.... I think I had cider – cider you could get at the supermarket for, I don't know, three bucks a gallon. And we were sitting around, listening to all the people singing about this and that, "Sweet Betsy From Pike," whatever. And then it was time for us to go, and they presented us with the bill, which was inCREDible. I mean, this tea, tea is what we saw, but they had 'Lapsang Souchong'...

"But if you sang, your stuff was free. So I said, 'I'll sing.' I got up, and I sang what my family recognized to be 'folk music.'"

Jackie Washington, as he would soon become known, is a hit that night. The calypso craze is still going strong, and Jack – smooth, confident, sexy, a reasonable incarnation of Harry Belafonte – is called back for encores.

Manny Greenhill is in the room, and he approaches Jack after the set. He sees Jack as someone who can command a room, whether a concert hall or a birthday party. Over the next few years, Jack will see plenty of both.

There is only one problem: Jackie Washington is a not such a hot guitar player. "Don't worry," Manny assures him. "My son will teach you."

And so I find myself mounting many stairs and maneuvering through a dark and seemingly endless hallway in Boston's South End. Jack is not that many years older than I, but he lives alone, in his own apartment! As I approach, a young woman is leaving, straightening her skirt.

Inside there are candles, hanging fabrics, and works of African art. Jack is friendly, charming even. He makes tea – from the supermarket this time, not Lapsang Souchong – and we get down to work.

His fingers are long and spidery, almost too long, if that's possible, and, as a reformed ukulele player, he is still getting used to the extra couple of strings. But I show him the basics of fingerpicking, much as Guy Carawan showed them to me. Merle Travis he is not, but we make some progress, and make a date to meet again.

Of all the relationships recalled in these pages, the one with Jack becomes most familial, despite its ebbs and flows over the years. It begins with dinners at Huntoon Street. When Jack comes, he picks a flower from our front lawn and presents it to my mother in a gesture that is simultaneously ironic and sincere. I love that! He comes often, almost a member of the household.

We are becoming more comfortable with each other, and in time I start to accompany him on guitar at some local performances. Jack sings, plays rhythm, and tells jokes; I take a few guitar solos between verses. By this time I have been working up a solo act of my own for anyone who will sit still – mostly the infirm and elderly, who have little choice in the matter. And in the summer of my seventeenth year, a big moment arrives – I go to Detroit with Jack, as both his accompanist and opening act. Excited, I consult the *Encyclopedia Brittanica* and become something of an expert on this exotic-sounding place, far to the west.

The reality is more prosaic. This club, the Coffee Gallery, lies in the section of Detroit's outskirts that Eminem will later make infamous as 8 Mile, rough and remote. But in the summer of 1961, it is largely Jewish, suburban and middle class. Proprietor Tzvi Wachtel, newly arrived from Israel, puts us up in the basement for our two-week engagement, and makes fun of the way we talk. "A gig, that's a

*Publicity for Expresso Night et al*

*Accompanying Jack in concert*

job, you know!" he screams, laughing uproariously. We hang out with like-minded young people, bent on having a good time and escaping from bourgeois America. I learn the basics of nightly entertainment, attend the Michigan State Fair, and finally lose my virginity.

Back home, I enter Harvard College, and continue to accompany Jack and to develop my musical skills. Much of this happens across the street from Harvard, at Club 47. I have a girlfriend now, and I no longer live at home.

A year or so later, Jack and I return to Detroit. This time we have a band, with bass and drums. We now play a new room called the Chessmate. Where the Golden Vanity imagines itself a ship, this room evokes a chessboard. Not only are the tablecloths black-and-white, but underneath them, hidden from sight, the tables are arranged black table/white table in eight rows.

The Detroit folk music scene has a reigning royal couple: Chuck and Joni Mitchell. One night, after the gig, they invite us to visit. Joni Mitchell has begun writing songs, and she sings us her new one, "Urge For Going." It's prescient; some months later, she's gone, leaving Detroit for warmer climes and wider vistas.

## 16-20 YEARS OLD : A WIDER WORLD WITH JACKIE WASHINGTON

*With Louise, Mississippi John Hurt and Jerry Ricks*

Jack and I also play the Second Fret in Philadelphia. Jerry Ricks, the cook and a good blues guitar player, becomes a friend. I will spend many nights at his various apartments, especially the big sunny one in Germantown. The club's owner Manny Rubin is a world-class complainer, and one night, after a litany of depressed moaning, he mounts the stairs to his office. And then suddenly – BAM! – a pistol shot rings out. We rush to his door, afraid of what we may find. Will Manny Rubin's brains be scattered over his desk? Will the cops come? Will we get paid?

But Manny has merely been indulging in target practice on some stuffed animal, whose feathery entrails, rather than Manny's brains, now adorn the walls and hang from lamps.

Jack and Jerry and I try to laugh it off, but the incident shakes me more than I hope I'm letting on. This road that I'm on, this journey deeper inside the music, is taking some unexpected twists and turns. I'm not sure how much I'm penetrating the music and its alluring secrets, but I'm surely getting a crash course into the music *business*, at least as it exists out in the cold wide world, rather than at warm and homey Folklore Productions – and it's a strange place. Does it make people nuts, or does it just attract nutty people?

Jack is helping me establish myself as a working musician, and simultaneously giving me the tools that I need to leave the home I grew up in and to establish my independence

At the same time, Jack is growing up himself and making a pretty good living in the music business. While I am working my way out of Dorchester, he takes a different path, buys a home back in Roxbury, near where he grew up. The house on Fort Hill has walls that date back to colonial times, when a real fort defended Boston. The band rehearses there for Jack's Vanguard album *Morning Song*. I accompany him at the Newport Folk Festival and eventually score my own slot there. As he assumes the role of the older brother I never had, showing me the ropes and keeping an eye on

*Accompanying Jack at Newport. Fritz Richmond on washtub bass*

*A typical month at Club 47*

my encounters with the wider world, my time with Jack becomes a time of expanded horizons.

But as I become more confident and find other mentors, I feel that I need Jack's protection less. With this, our family ties lessen somewhat. But I continue to join him for dinners at 4 Huntoon Street, where his connection to my parents remains strong, and I continue to play in his band through 1965 and into 1966. We perform at the 47 and the Unicorn in Boston and at a number of clubs in the east and Midwest. The birth of my son Matthew revives our familial ebb-and-flow in a new dynamic. Jack says the kid looks like Winston Churchill and feels a caretaking responsibility to keep the band working, help keep food on my expanding family's table. Louise and child travel with us to Ottawa for an engagement at Le Hibou. Mattie is a squirming squawking handful by now, nearly a year old and crawling every which way. The performances run late and he wakes up early. One day the sun breaks through the Ontario gloom, and Louise and I wearily take Mattie to the riverbank, where he crawls through a Wordsworthian field of golden daffodils.

*Leona, Eric, Jack*

The band also plays a few rooms outside its normal comfort zone. Like the strip joint in Allston, where we share the bill with Chinky and her Fabulous Tassels. I'm surprised to find that I am able to walk to this gig, just across the Charles River from my Cambridge digs on Kinnaird Street. As I step across the Anderson Bridge, guitar case in hand, the Harvard Rowing Team is practicing its strokes. In physical distance, the strip joint lies not much farther from home than Club 47. But in another sense, it's worlds away. At one point the master of ceremonies emerges from

Chinky's dressing room, grumbling "I can't get it up." Not the kind of talk one hears in Club 47's back room. Chinky herself is a wistful, somewhat philosophical lady who talks proudly about her daughter's achievements at school. I sit in with the band a couple of times, as she undresses for the none-too-sober crowd, among whom there is little evidence either of Pete Seeger's flannel shirts or of Miles Davis' sharp suits.

I spend a while longer in the Boston-Cambridge music scene, then head to California. By then I am an adult of sorts: a husband and a father of two children.

Jack and I maintain sporadic contact over the years. When I play the Bitter End in New York with my new partner Mayne Smith, Jack shows up in the audience. He is an actor now, and I see him perform at the Public Theater. Eventually he too reaches California, where we accept our status as elders while resuming a relationship informed by our half-century of history.

In early 2011, my mother is 92 years old. She lies on her deathbed in an assisted living facility in Santa Monica. I bring my guitar to sing her some songs, ease her passage, perhaps bring some pleasant memories. Pausing outside her room, I hear another guitar and another voice singing. It is Jack, with the same idea. He has been there a while, and now starts to pack up and move on. As I move into the chair next to her bed, I remark, "I used to open for you, back in the day." I'm thinking about the Chessmate, the Second Fret, and the raft of

*Leona Greenhill*

east coast coffeehouses. "Now you're opening for me."

"Yeah," Jack replies, "But this is your town."

Some weeks later, in late spring, we are back in Boston, overlooking the Charles River, for a memorial service. Jack's stories are funny and sad, and then the Silver Leaf Gospel Quintet joins to send Leona Greenhill off. We scatter her ashes in the Boston Public Garden and in the Charles River – a last request to defy authority, to break the rules.

*Pete Seeger sends regrets*

# THE BIG CITY
## New York

Not that long ago, images of baseball heroes adorned my bedroom wall – Jackie Robinson, PeeWee Reese. At my first baseball game, Brooklyn Dodgers versus the Boston Braves, I heard PeeWee tell a fan to go to hell. (Wow! He not only talks, he swears.) I would frequent Fenway Park and listen on my portable radio – sometimes surreptitiously in my bed, after I was supposed to be asleep – to the Red Sox, who were gradually winning my allegiance.

But now my heroes are blues singers – Robert Johnson, Skip James, Bessie Smith. At night, if atmospheric conditions are right, my radio can pick up John R from WLAC in Nashville; he plays everything from B.B. King to Jimmy Reed. I snuggle under the covers in my flannel pajamas and commune as deeply as I can with these distant sounds.

I devour the available recordings, especially Sam Char-

*Barbecue Bob, preparing to cook*

ters's anthology *The Country Blues*, the book as well as the album. It is Charters who turns me on to Barbecue Bob, a Georgia musician with a powerful 12-string guitar style.

In 1960, recordings of such an obscure musician are hard to find. But fortunately the blues underground reveals a source, a record shop in midtown Manhattan. This place doesn't sell actual vinyl recordings; instead it sells metal acetates, of blues singers whose work is otherwise unavailable.

An acetate recording is not designed to last. It is designed, rather, as a reference, before one commits to pressing a run of vinyl. As soon as the needle hits its groove, the acetate starts a quick descent into oblivion. The fruit fly's life cycle is maybe twenty-eight days; the acetate's is about ten plays. After that, scratchy white noise drowns out music – it sounds like a rainstorm on your windshield, so hard that you can't see the road – and you have to give up.

I learn that for twenty dollars – a considerable investment for a mid-twentieth century American teenager – I can acquire an acetate of Barbecue Bob singing maybe ten songs. Or maybe his entire recorded works. Or maybe the two lists are identical.

So one weekend I arrange to stay with "Uncle" Steve Gardner, and take the Greyhound bus to New York. I make my way from Port Authority Bus Terminal to the store, somewhere in the 50s, fork over my twenty bucks, and leave with the acetate under my arm.

Over the next few years, I do this several times, as my panoply of heroes and the store's inventory both expand. I don't know where these acetates are now,

*Mr. Barbecue Bob, more formally attired*

probably in some landfill. But I do know that I learn to listen with an intensity that in future decades, when the world's music will be an easy mouse-click away, I will no longer be able to summon. With each play, the music on the disc grows fainter, until, like Elvis some years later, it has left the building. As it drifts away into the sonic fog, I listen that much harder and try to replace the fading notes with ones of my own.

So Barbecue Bob gets me to New York as a solo traveler. As I grow into my later teens and become more independent, my trips to New York expand. My wanderlust takes me uptown to catch rhythm-and-blues extravaganzas at the Apollo Theater, where the house band ignores any boundaries between soul music and jazz. On one amazing day, Jimmy Reed is the opening act for B.B. King. If Reed and King are just a subway ride away, I've got to be there. While I feel like a visitor to Harlem, whose culture is a good deal different from Dorchester's, I feel pretty much at home in the rhythm-and-blues community, for whom the Apollo is church. Outside on 125th Street I'm the object of questioning, even suspicious glances. Inside the theater I'm just one of a thousand people digging Jimmy Reed and B.B. King. We're reacting together, even exchanging comments with each other or the stage. This is the world to which John R and WLAC, Sam Charters and Barbecue Bob, have been beckoning me.

I stay for two shows. Reed seems drunk and uninspired, especially in the second show, where he more or less goes through the motions. King, on the other hand, is on fire, his creative juices flowing generously. His guitar solos in the second show are much different from those in the first show, a revelation. For him, the guitar neck no longer hides any obstacles, but is instead fully under his command. It is the first of several times that I will get my batteries recharged by the Blues Boy, including late in his life, when he no longer stands to perform. Even then, he makes the music happen, and never phones it in.

Down in Greenwich Village, a number of music and poetry rooms vie for trade from both tourists and locals. The poetry rooms, especially, place a premium on in-your-face, sassy transgressions. One poet declaims, "I smell an elephant shitting. It must be John Foster Dulles dying."

My favorite Village haunt is the Gaslight, in a basement on MacDougal Street. Clarence Hood, a Mississippi expat with a courtly, somewhat patrician affect, is the proprietor. Dave Van Ronk hosts the open mic nights. He lives upstairs, on the third floor, and keeps his seat in an ongoing poker game on the second floor. When he draws a weak hand, he conveniently recalls that he needs to introduce the next act, and retreats to the basement stage.

> *I had a dream that the Gaslight was clean and*
> *the rats were all scrubbed down*
> *The coffee was great and the waitresses straight, and*
> *Patrick Sky left town*
> *No one was swacked and Dylan played Bach, and*
> *Ochs's songs all scanned*
> *I got out of bed and straightened my head, and*
> *started a rock-and-roll band*
> *– Dave Van Ronk*

On the ground floor, between the Gaslight and the poker game, is the Kettle of Fish. In this neighborhood watering hole, some of the scene's sharpest and most sarcastic wits – Phil Ochs, Bob Dylan, Albert Grossman, Tom Paxton, as well as Van Ronk – trade barbs in high-stakes intellectual combat. Sometimes they argue about politics – Dave is a Trotskyite whose Jesuit upbringing stands him in good stead as he defends what is probably the farthest left bastion, against, say, Dylan's less rigorous approach. ("Bobby was not really a political person," Dave will later reflect. "We thought he was hopelessly naïve politically. But in retrospect I think he may have been more sophisticated than we were.") And sometimes they argue about art, including the combatants' latest songwriting efforts. In either case, woe to the person who comes unprepared to defend his point of view, or hasn't fully thought it through.

Although my chops in the realm of conversation as a blood sport are not at his level, Dave takes a liking to me. Maybe it's because we share both an affinity for and a relationship with Reverend Gary Davis. Or maybe it's the aftermath of our chug-a-lug contest, in which Dave suckers me into a bet on who can first finish three steins of beer. The six libations are set before us on a table. I sort of hold my own through the first glass. But before I am halfway through my second, Dave is well into his third, and the game is done. After thoroughly trouncing me, Dave turns solicitous. It was foolish of me to agree to the wager, he instructs, his Jesuit analytical skills again surfacing. But I survived with dignity and he won't take advantage again. And he never does. Burping after this rite of passage, I am now invited into the group. Eventually I manage to recoup a modicum of status by winning my own bet – on baseball, of course – from the formidable Albert Grossman. I leave with the mogul's three dollars. I doubt that this figures as even a rounding error to the manager of Bob Dylan and Peter Paul & Mary; but to me it feels pretty big.

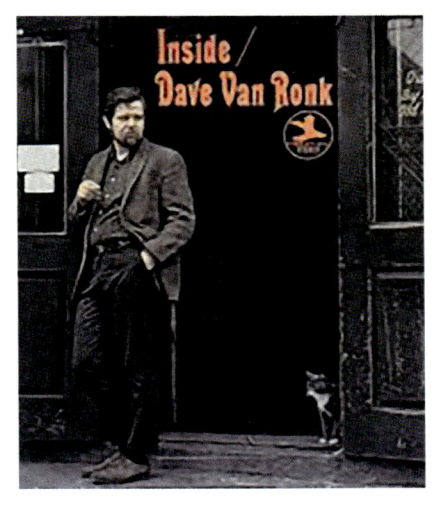

*Van Ronk at the Kettle of Fish*

Dave invites me downstairs to contribute a few tunes on the Gaslight's stage. It's a different scene from the 47 and the Unicorn up north. Here a substantial portion of the audience is comprised of tourists, curious to see real beatniks. And couples from uptown, slumming, showing that they know their way below 14th Street. I dig in and try to show that I know my way around the blues.

After a number of open mic appearances, and hanging with Van Ronk and his court, and maybe (who knows?) with some unacknowledged help from my dad, I eventually graduate to a two-week engagement as opening act to Jesse Fuller, whom Folklore Productions represents.

Jesse, in his musical and personal history, somewhat resembles Barbecue Bob. Both were born in rural Georgia around the turn of the century, and both play old, almost forgotten forms of the blues. But while Barbecue Bob died in 1931, Jesse Fuller is very much alive, with a smile that won't quit and a strong sense of himself. He stands tall, feet planted firmly on the ground, comfortable in his own skin.

He's also a bit like Reverend Davis, another emissary from the nineteenth century. They personally knew people, probably including their grandparents, who had been slaves. And like Davis, he hears a bigger sound in his mind. But where Davis has followed that muse by creating an expansive guitar style that he calls "playing the piano," Fuller has formed a one-man band for himself: not only does he sing and play twelve-string guitar, but he also incorporates harmonica and kazoo, which he keeps side-by-side on a rack around his neck. Bass notes are provided by the "fotdella," an instrument of his own devising, which he plays with his feet.

Jesse's sense of self-sufficiency goes beyond his stage presentation. It's not for nothing that he is called the Lone Cat. In New York,

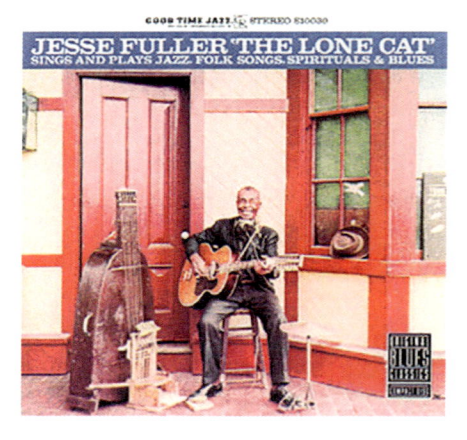

*Jesse Fuller's one-man band*

when we finish our sets at the Gaslight, Jesse politely declines numerous offers of places to sleep. Instead, he aims his station wagon north to Central Park, where he stretches out and retires for the night. "I always go by myself," he says.

The vehicle is essential to Jesse's sense of himself and how he sees himself in the world. On Memorial Day he goes by himself to the Indianapolis 500 auto race. He will not accept a booking that conflicts with this sacred obligation. It's the only herd that he follows.

As Black Power grows in politics and culture, Jesse is sometimes derided for playing music, like the sort that accompanies his buck-and-wing dance steps, that harkens back to minstrel days. He makes no apology but is instead proud of his art. It's interesting to visit him at home in Oakland. He lives around the corner from the Black Panthers, who are gaining a following with a philosophy of armed self-defense against racism. They are from different worlds, but Jesse Fuller and the Panthers somehow manage to get along just fine.

*Jesse Fuller*

Back in New York, at the Gaslight, Jesse wraps up his set with "I Double Double Do Love You" or "Hanging 'Round the Skin Game" or probably "San Francisco Bay Blues," his most famous song, which will be covered by the likes of Eric Clapton and Paul McCartney. Packing up our gear in our shared tiny dressing room, we develop a simple choreography to avoid bumping into one another. He packs up his twelve-string guitar, moves his fotdella to a safe corner, and together we climb the stairs to MacDougal Street.

Through the Kettle of Fish's big picture window, Dylan, Van Ronk and the other culture warriors are still arguing a passionate point about Phil Ochs's new song or the war in Vietnam. A light rain is falling, and Jesse buttons up his fleece jacket against the midnight chill. We walk together for a block or two – I to the A Train, he to his station wagon. Unlike Lightnin' Hopkins, Jesse Fuller needs no driver. We say good night until tomorrow, and I descend the subway steps, heading towards "Uncle" Steve's. Jesse opens the station wagon door and sits for a moment in the front seat, home at last. He places the twelve-string next to his open bedroll. He turns the key, and slowly, carefully makes his way north, up Sixth Avenue to Central Park. Of all the park's feral felines, this Lone Cat may be the most independent, the most free.

*Jesse Fuller demonstrates the buck-and-wing to Manny Greenhill, James Cotton and CBC television crew*

# THE BIG COUNTRY
*Inside of the Outside*

On my first day at Harvard College I meet Jim Field, as he moves into the room next to mine. He's a tow-headed teenager, about a year older than me, from Boston's North Shore. At first I think he is one of "them," the strange prep-school tribe that speaks a deeply encoded language of entitled privilege. But I soon learn that his background is closer to my own, middle-class secular Jewish. I get his jokes and he gets mine, a language rooted in pastrami sandwiches from Katz's Delicatessen. We also share a love for southern mountain music, which we both play and seek, like a treasure. When we're not hanging out at Club 47, we play music in his dorm room or mine. I'm trying to get a handle on Earl Scruggs's three-finger banjo style, while Jim is developing his high lonesome vocals. We spend a good deal of time listening to recordings by the Stanley Brothers, who seem to combine the music's rough and polished elements.

In our sophomore year, Jim and I embark on a musical adventure. Skipping a couple of classes, we cut out early on a Friday, stick out our thumbs, and hitchhike south towards Galax, Virginia. There we hope to catch most of the Galax Old Fiddlers Convention, established in 1935. Galax is just across the Shenandoah Valley from where the Stanley Brothers grew up, and we are eager to breathe the same mountain air that sustained them.

As always, the hitchhiking goes more slowly than we had hoped. But we score some long hauls and reach Galax in the middle of the night. With a youthful flexibility that I now can only marvel at, we stretch out by the side of the road and, to the faint hooting of a distant owl, fall asleep.

Hours later, a peppier family of birds begins to intrude on my slumber, and a too-bright shaft of sunlight hits my eyelids. I bury my head in my jacket, hug my guitar a little tighter, and try to delay waking for a bit longer. But then I hear a voice. "Are you boys okay?" And I open my eyes to see, in the first light of dawn, an honest-to-god Southern bluegrass band, dressed in matching white suits. Jim, a bit more awake than I, rises to his feet and begins to explain our situation to the leader. He in turn examines with curiosity our long hair, my beard, the cut of our tight-at-the-ankle jeans, and Jim's pointy Filippo Verde boots from Italy. "Where are you boys from?" he asks. Chuckling, he adds, "Well I know you're Yankees, but from where exactly?"

A few minutes later we have piled our instruments on top of theirs and crammed into the band's station wagon. We are on our way to their first gig of the day, a rise-and-shine radio show. The band's job is to provide a cheerful musical background to morning chores. Perhaps the rapid bluegrass tempos lead to faster milking? Whatever the aim, we feel suddenly on the inside of the outside, right where we belong.

Okay, so they're not the Stanley Brothers, but they are the real deal, and far removed from the citybilly *manqués* trying to recreate the music in northern coffeehouses. A ways into the program, the band members all crowd around the single microphone to sing, in four-part harmony, the hymn "Precious Memories." Jim and I know it from the Stanley Brothers recording. But when the band reaches the crucial line, "Sacred scenes unfold," they instead sing of "sacred *seams*." Jim and I look at each other, grin a bit, then come upon the same thought: maybe it's better this way, more poetic.

The festival itself gets started around noon, with local bands, both amateur and semi-professional. The quality varies, but these people have grown up with this music, and it's clear that their connection is innate rather than acquired. As the festival progresses, so does the music. By evening, the focus is on instrumental contests. We are surprised and thrilled to see the great Clarence "Tom" Ashley, known to us from his iconic rendition of "The Coo Coo Bird" on Harry Smith's *Anthology of American Folk Music*, appear out of the Blue Ridge

*Clarence "Tom" Ashley*

mist to enter the banjo clawhammer contest. And soon, there he is, actually singing "The Coo Coo" into the breezy night sky and frailing the banjo, striking down on the strings with his fingernails. He's playing in a modal tuning, the melody comprised of only five notes, almost like Lightnin' Hopkins's blues scale. It's a mysterious song that juxtaposes the bird with the singer's boasts of his gambling prowess.

*Oh the coo coo, she's a pretty bird,*
   *She warbles as she flies*
*She never hollers 'coo coo'*
   *Til the fourth day of July*

*I've played cards in England,*
   *I've played cards in Spain*
*I'll bet you ten dollars*
   *I'll beat you next game*

Jim and I are enthralled. We have struck gold! He sounds even better than on the record – grittier, more real. Maybe it's all the living he's experienced since that 1929 recording, when he was in his early thirties, performing in medicine shows. Now in his late sixties, his music carries a history in every note.

Dear Winnie Winston,

So sorry to hear of your death, far off in New Zealand. Got me to thinking of our times together, from Galax (where you won the frailing contest over Tom Ashley!), to playing in bands behind Rosalie Sorrels, to hanging out in Cajun Country. There I was visiting Marc and Ann Savoy, and you were playing pedal steel behind Dewey Balfa at a Mardi Gras gig in Basile. Here's to you, your expansive musical tastes and skills. All will be missed.

  Dewey Balfa — I first heard him at the Newport Folk Festival. We over-educated city kids felt privileged to get a rare glimpse into genuine Cajun culture, which I assumed to be highly prized back home in Louisiana. But in Basile, Dewey told me just how important that Newport appearance was for him and for Cajun culture as a whole. "Ten thousand people stood up and cheered," he recalled, and that gave him and his compatriots permission to walk a little taller back home, to take pride in a culture that was in danger of fading away before the forces of modernity.

My "Dear Winnie" letter

Unknown, Susan Krebs, Mitch, Ann and Marc Savoy, Winnie. Eunice LA, Mardi Gras 1983

But the judges, perhaps not considering Ashley's rendition flashy enough, give first prize to Winnie Winston, who, like us, has made his way here from up north.

The Galax Festival reaches a climax on Saturday night, with the more modern bluegrass style – "folk music with overdrive" – overshadowing Tom Ashley's old-time approach. And our new friends, who plucked us from our roadside slumber, acquit themselves well, thanks partly to a good turnout from their radio audience.

Next morning, Jim and I are eating eggs and grits at a local restaurant. We now seem to be the only northerners in Galax, and have become something of a curiosity to the locals, many of whom are dressed for church. They seem particularly interested in Jim's granny glasses, which are becoming hip in Cambridge but in Appalachia are reserved for actual grandmothers. The waitress keeps filling our coffee cups, the first time I've experienced that ritual; in Harvard Square, the Hayes-Bickford makes you buy every cup. Everybody knows that we're aliens of some sort, but it's cool, we're tolerated. At times we even feel like we belong.

Maybe it's this sense of successful entry or maybe it's a misplaced confidence in our hitchhiking karma that leads Jim and me to decide to take the longer, more scenic route home. Sticking out our thumbs, we quickly hitch a ride west, across the Shenandoah Valley and the mountain ridge that forms its western border. But our progress slows somewhat in East Tennessee. We spend several hours in Sevierville, where a waif in a smudgy shift wanders up from her yard to ask, "Cain't uns get a ride?" We eventually do hitch out of Sevierville, but we hit a wall just outside of Lynch, Kentucky, in a mountainous stretch that is poor, isolated, and suspicious of strangers. No one gives us a ride. As night falls, we decide to walk along the winding and hilly road that blocks our progress. Maybe around the next bend, things will be better.

Thick woods hug close by the road and block out the moonlight. We can hear crickets and night birds, maybe an owl. And from somewhere in front of us, not yet visible, comes the sound of a car, going very fast. Suddenly it appears, right in front of us. We leap to the roadside, out of its path. The car too swerves, with a screech of brakes and tires. From the front seat, somebody yells something, and it is not a hospitable pleasantry. In fact, it sounds like a threat. Did he say something about coming back to kill us?

Really scared now, we scramble off that stretch of road, and hide in a clump of bushes. We stay there a long time, until the big moon lights the hillside and we start to overcome our anxiety. With our heart rates approaching normal, we walk farther. After half a mile or so, we come upon two dump trucks parked side by side. I crawl into the cab of one, Jim into the other, and we manage a couple of hours of fitful sleep

We wake with the first hint of dawn. As sunlight starts to find the tallest trees, Jim and I unpack our instruments and play a lonesome tune by the side of the road. Notes languidly rouse themselves from our instruments and drift into the fading Kentucky mist. We don't know whether today's travel will be smoother or not. But we do have a new sense of the music that was missing up north, in our dormitory. Maybe we'll figure how to get inside this music, after all, as it has gotten inside us. As the notes bounce off the pickup trucks and into the tall trees, I manage a smile. I look over at Jim and say, "It sounds better down here." He responds with a classic riff in G position.

# THE BIG WORLD
*Larger Struggles*

In early 1962 the Freedom Singers come to town for a fundraising concert. Bernice Johnson and her husband-to-be Cordell Reagon stay at our house. Bernice at this point is some years away from her evolution into Dr. Bernice Johnson Reagon of the Smithsonian Institution, Howard University and Sweet Honey in the Rock; but you can tell that she's bound to scale mountains.

*The Freedom Singers: Bernice Johnson, Cordell Reagon, Charles Neblett, and Rutha Harris*

The Freedom Singers are fresh from the dangerous civil rights campaign in Albany, Georgia. They sing songs of the struggle, not only "We Shall Overcome," which I've heard from Pete Seeger and Guy Carawan, but also "This Little Light Of Mine," with words somewhat altered from how I remember Sister Rosetta Tharpe singing it, and "Ain't Gonna Let Nobody Turn Me Around." Emissaries to liberal allies up north, the Freedom Singers are unfailingly polite and approachable, but you can tell that, at some level, they see the world as divided between those who live their politics in the streets and those who don't.

Although I am among the latter, I am asked to open the concert, held in a church in Boston's Back Bay neighborhood, with a brief set of my own. It's a bit of a struggle to justify, including to myself, where I fit. On the one hand, I have been demonstrating for a long time. My mother tells me she pushed me in a baby carriage as she marched to support leftist legislator Vito Marcantonio. As a high school student, I picketed Woolworth's Department Store on Tremont Street, because of its segregation policy in southern states. (It was confusing to see Negro shoppers, as they were then termed, cross the picket line to take advantage of a January sale.) And when racism hits close to home, as when Jackie Washington is beaten bloody, his nose broken by a Boston policeman, I'm with the local music community in his support. (Jack is eventually acquitted of the charge "being abroad at night"; the cops get off scot-free.)

But those are safe actions, taken with familiar allies on the streets of my hometown. I feel it's time to go farther. So in 1963, inspired by the Freedom Singers and others, I take a bus to Cambridge, Maryland, to help register voters with the Congress of Racial Equality. As the bus rolls into the Eastern Shore, an area whose culture is closer to the deep south than to Baltimore or Washington, I'm imagining physical danger and perhaps jail. My brave chants against racism seem a thin and shaky antidote to my fear.

But the reality is more prosaic. Instead of jail, CORE first assigns me to carry voter registration forms from door to door. The dwellings are mostly single wood-frame structures, and the people, while polite, have either already signed up earlier in the drive or are reluctant to do so. After a few days of this I am next stationed at the local pool hall, which, I'm told, is stocked with potential voters. The tables are in fairly good shape, with a minimum of cigarette burns on the rails and beer stains on the felt. By the second day, I'm getting a feel for the place, and my pool game improves somewhat. I can't recall how many voters I register, but I learn how to leave the cue ball near a corner where the wall stands close to a table, to my opponent's disadvantage.

I share a spare bedroom with another white volunteer in a local woman's home. At one point she asks us, "Don't you ever feel like going downtown, to mingle with your own kind?" As if Maryland's Eastern Shore contains a cadre of local over-educated Jewish liberals. But race is such a clear and overwhelming divide, I almost understand what she means.

I spend maybe ten days in Cambridge, adding my small contribution to the larger struggle. And later that summer I join the March On Washington, where rumor has it that Martin Luther King gives one hell of a speech. But by the time that Reverend King speaks, I'm wandering away from the Lincoln Memorial, feeling the effects of my all-night hitchhike. Especially the last ride — a big black Cadillac filled with big black men generously sharing a big black bottle of Johnny Walker — all the way from the George Washington Bridge to the march in D.C. And besides, I've already heard my hero John Lewis, whose speech, we later learn, is severely compromised so as not to lose the more establishment-oriented of the march's organizers.

Not that I totally miss Martin Luther King's oratory. In my early teenage years, about the time that my mother brings me to hear Sister Rosetta Tharpe, she also brings me to hear Reverend King speak at a small gathering in Roxbury. Here he is low-key, more the community organizer than the charismatic leader.

That role more befits Malcolm X, whom I hear preach to a gathering of thousands at the Boston Arena – which I know more familiarly as the venue for high-school hockey games, triple headers pitting rivals like Southie versus Eastie, or Latin versus English.

I go alone to hear Malcolm argue against King's non-violent approach. I make my way to the second balcony, where mine is the only white face in a sea of brown and black. Caught up in the cadences and passion of his delivery, I find myself cheering Malcolm's condemnation of white devils. My neighbors are amused, but the event's security attendants – all black suits with skinny lapels, clean-shaven, short hair – are not. They ask me either to leave or to move down front with the press and the rest of the "observers." I take offense, and walk out – probably what they want – but not before I get a good dose of Malcolm, easily the most powerful orator I will ever experience.

The Boston Arena, now long gone, is also where I attend sublime concerts by James Brown in his prime, and a host of other guiding lights of African-American culture. The South End is, in fact, one area of Boston, a city divided into ethnic fiefdoms, where the races meet and commingle. A few blocks away from the Arena is the South End School of Music, scene of my early piano lessons. One block in the other direction is Symphony Hall, home of the Boston Symphony Orchestra and the bastion of "high" culture. Down the hill is the Hi-Hat, a classy nightclub where touring rhythm-and-blues artists like Joe Tex and Wilson Pickett land. (One night Jackie Washington, seated next to me, is introduced from the stage as a local folksinger. "Hey, does that music have a beat?" the MC wisecracks.) And nearby is one of the two local musicians' unions, the black one, which I join – partly out of solidarity with a culture I'm learning to identify with, and partly because of the cheaper dues and initiation fee.

In addition to civil rights, the other issue that compels attention is the war in Vietnam. The first war casualty whom I knew personally was Lou Walling, who hosted the radio program "Hillbilly At Harvard" on campus station WHRB. This was back in my high school days, before Americans knew that their army was fighting. Rolf Cahn pointed it out to me and predicted worse to come. By the time I am a college student, the war has escalated and is a topic of intense concern. My sophomore roommate Wilson Halley eventually volunteers, is wounded, goes back for another tour, and is killed.

I support historian H. Stuart Hughes's anti-Vietnam War campaign for the U.S. Senate against the entitled rookie Ted Kennedy, but am disappointed in Hughes' intellectual history course. (Kennedy somehow manages to survive my opposition and flourish.) Another prominent academic, Stanley Hoffman, is rumored to be under consideration for Secretary of State until he finally decides to declare his opposition to the war. (Like many of his other students, I wonder what took him so long.)

The war is a constant presence. Our college enrollment keeps us out of the draft, at least for the time being. But there are constant protests and discussions. I join Tocsin, an anti-war group led by senior Todd Gitlin, who will later emerge as an incisive social commentator from academia. Even then, Todd is a natural leader, moderating some intense discussions during the Cuban Missile Crisis of 1962.

In 1963 the war in Vietnam becomes more intense, and I join a number of demonstrations. We merely march, but in Saigon, Buddhist monks are now setting themselves on fire. In early November, when President Diem of South Vietnam is assassinated, my group believes reports that the United States has condoned the coup. But when President Kennedy is assassinated a few weeks later, we don't know what to think. Louise and I having temporarily parted ways, I am on a weekend date with a potential new girlfriend. She and I huddle close to the confusing news reports. We don't really know each other well enough to provide solace, but we have nowhere else to turn, and I gain new understanding of the old saying: *any port in a storm*. When I drop her off at her Brandeis University dormitory, nightclub owner Jack Ruby has just pumped several bullets into Lee Harvey Oswald as that prisoner is escorted through a jail corridor. Eyes on the black-and-white TV screen, one student, perhaps trying to shrink the events into something he can grasp, mutters, "Of course a Jew would have to be involved!"

By 1964 my commitment to political action begins to ebb a bit. Jack and I plan to join Freedom Summer in Mississippi. It seems a good follow-up to my stint the year before in Cambridge, Maryland, and the March On Washington. But by now my romance with Louise Rice has reached the point of no return, and we get married instead. It signals a loosening of ties between Jack and me. While I do not regret my marriage and the two precious children who follow, I do come to regret having left too soon, not participating in the summer's historic events. Instead, I find myself in the gallery of the House of Representatives, as the Voting Rights Act is passed. I'm in a ringside seat rather than in the streets.

*I always say goodbye too soon*
*I'm thinking divorce on the honeymoon*
*I step back to check how I'm doin'*
*And say goodbye too soon*
— *Mitch Greenhill*

## 17-22 YEARS OLD

*Geoff Muldaur's School of Hip, and the
Cambridge-Boston Music Scene*

For those of us who follow this music, the Newport Folk Festival is the pinnacle of the year. That's where, in 1959, Joan Baez steps into the spotlight and becomes a star. Poor Bob Gibson, the well-established folksinger who has invited her to join him on one song, is left in her dust. Nobody can take their eyes off the beautiful barefoot girl with the haunting soprano.

Newport is where Bob Dylan establishes himself as king of the

*Bob Gibson, Joan Baez, Newport 1959*

singer-songwriters and heir to his idol Woody Guthrie. It's where the New York and Cambridge-Boston scenes meet on neutral ground to wage musical combat, fret to fret, pick to pick. (Is Eric von Schmidt's blues more real than Dave Van Ronk's?) And crucially, it's where we city folk get to hear and interact with musicians from deep in rural America, who created this music.

At Newport, the evening concerts are held in a stadium, where spotlights and a strong sound system send the performances out to an audience of thousands. The more intimate workshops are held at the posh Newport Tennis Club, down the road from mansions where the cream of American capitalism has summered for 100 years. In short, the Newport Folk Festival is a very big deal.

At the other end of the food chain, the Folksong Society of Greater Boston hosts hootenannies in the basement of the YMCA on Huntington Avenue. The linoleum floor is a bit sticky and you can smell chlorine from the swimming pool.

There's a pot of coffee in the corner, and somebody has baked cookies. In a circle of folding chairs, people take turns leading the group in song, or in singing ballads and other folk songs. For a while, murder ballads are popular, then Woody Guthrie's union anthems:

> *There once was a union maid,*
> *Who never was afraid*
> *Of goons and ginks and company finks*
> *And deputy sheriffs who made the raid*

The men favor blue jeans, heavy boots and knit sweaters that evoke Irish fishermen. Their hair has begun to creep over their ears. A number of women, many with hair down to their waists, sport ethnic peasant dresses in the Eastern European style. At some point, one will pick a gentle arpeggio on her guitar and sing, in a sweet clear soprano:

*The water is wide, I cannot cross over*
*And neither have I wings to fly*
*Build me a boat that can carry two*
*And both shall row, my love and I*

I've been attending these gatherings for several years. On the one hand, it's a world where I'm fully accepted, and I like that. And I like its democracy – all are welcome and encouraged to participate. On the other hand, the predictability is starting to wear thin.

And then one day, a new guy shows up. He's dressed more prep school than proletarian wannabe. His shirt has a button-down collar. His shoes have been recently shined and his hair is cut defiantly short, well above his ears.

Just in from his hometown of Princeton, New Jersey, Geoff Muldaur picks up a guitar and launches into a ribald song about jelly roll.

*Mr. Jelly Roll Baker,*
*let me be your slave*
*When Gabriel blows his trumpet,*
*gonna rise from my grave*
*For some of your sweet jelly, I love*
*your jelly roll*

His powerful voice, marked by a distinctive vibrato that I will vainly attempt to imitate, fills the room and takes focus. And the subject matter – way more sexually explicit than the group is used to – scandalizes a few attendees, especially those with children. I hear somebody whisper that he shouldn't be singing

*Geoff Muldaur*

that song here. But I am charmed. I can now pick up the innuendos better than I did a few years ago, when Sonny Terry slyly sang about a key that no longer fit a lock.

Geoff is a few months older than I, but still much closer to my own age, on the border between adolescence and maturity, than the adults who inhabit both this room and the larger local music scene. He has arrived to attend Boston University, but soon drops out and takes a job at Massachusetts General Hospital, the night shift. In gory detail, he tells bloody stories about cleaning up the operating room, daring you to react. He rents an apartment on Massachusetts Avenue in Cambridge, between Central and Harvard Squares, which means between town and gown. Mesmerized by his musicianship, charisma, and aura of hipness, I hang out there as often as I can. I'm happy to become his protégé, to be pulled along in his slipstream.

As we become friends, he sets out to fill gaps in my musical education. If I'm to be moving alongside him, I had better shape up and learn who's great and who's a phony. He parses the words that Skip James, long lost delta bluesman, rolls around in his Mississippi mouth.

> *I'd rather be the devil to be my woman's man*
> *Nothing but the devil change my baby's mind*

Does he mean he'd rather be the devil *than* to be his woman's man? Or does he mean he's *got* to be the devil to be the woman's man? Next cut is Skip's "Hard Time Killing Floor Blues":

> *If I ever can get up off of this old hard killin' floor*
> *Lord, I'll never get down this low no more*

That song leads to our first fight. Not about the words, which are clear enough. But when I sing the melody, Geoff finds a crucial mistake. He sings it back to me, but I can't tell the difference. He gets angry and I try again. Then I get angry, frustrated that he's picking on me, being stubborn. Finally I manage to sing it to his satisfaction, and we make up and move on. He wants to teach me how to hear jazz.

Django Reinhardt is on the turntable. "Did you get that?" Geoff instructs, as we listen closely to the guitar solo on "La Mer." "Do you hear how Django implies that note, the top of the triad, rather than play it? By playing the first two notes, he's making you hear something that's not actually there, making you hear a phantom note." Yes, once Geoff points it out, I can hear it. In later years, I'll hear Beethoven do much the same.

We light up a joint and listen to Ravi Shankar, Ali Akbar Khan and Alla Rakha play a morning raga. The structure of this music is beyond our comprehension, but we are content to bathe in the pure, intense sound of the sitar, sarod and tabla. Geoff says that a master tabla player like Alla Rakha has to study for years before his teacher will allow him even to pick up the instrument. First he has to become expert at singing the drum's notes and patterns. Geoff illustrates by riffing what sounds just like the complex tabla pattern that we just heard:

*Dha DhiNaKa GaKiTa DhiNaKa*
*Dha TiRaKiTa DhaTiTa DhiNaGa DhiGiNa*

As I chase Geoff down this rabbit hole of musical wonder, I feel changes in my hearing. If my ears were a camera, it would feel like the aperture was opening ever wider, letting in more light. Or maybe I'm just a country bumpkin recently arrived in Hip City, struggling to keep up.

Although Geoff has dropped out, I'm still very much the college student, with papers to write and tests to study for. After I move off campus, Geoff takes to stopping by in the afternoon, when I'm ready to take a break from homework. These studies

*Playing with Geoff Muldaur, some years later*

are sometimes tedious, at other times really interesting. I've always had a feel for academics, and am starting to understand Harvard's version. But either way, I'm happy to put a bookmark in the chapter and pick up a guitar instead. Often Geoff brings his clarinet. His clarinet playing is not on a par with his singing and guitar work, but he can move comfortably around the home key of B flat, and has a great feel for phrasing. After a couple of hours, he's off on his rounds of hipness, and I find my bookmark and pick up where I left off.

From my professors at Harvard – academic heavyweights like Crane Brinton and Oscar Handlin – I'm learning intellectual history of the eighteenth and nineteenth centuries. From Geoff I'm learning, first, the skill of listening to music; and second, the art of hanging out. His lessons are as rigorous as Harvard's – and, because they're more abstract, harder. Both the Harvard faculty and Geoff can make me feel three inches tall when I screw up, but they have different styles. When my essay takes a wrong turn, one graduate student who grades papers responds with a rubber stamp that screams "OH NO!" Geoff's response, if I say or like something unhip – like the time I impulsively burst into the kids' song "Marching to Pretoria" – is less direct but equally cutting. "Ah yes," he nods, "summer camp."

But on the few occasions when he gives praise – especially when I come up with a guitar phrase that he deems worthy – I am transported to a realm of enormous validation that a Harvard 'A' can't match. His path is strict, and it seems he's always right. Geoff has an unerring ear that just can't accept what it can't accept, and an appreciation of excellence. All of which make for tough lessons in musical discrimination.

Geoff quickly makes his way to the center of the Cambridge-Boston music scene. He performs regularly at Club 47. And when Paul Rothchild moves from the 47's front desk to a position at Prestige Records in New York, he taps Geoff to be among the first in our crowd to make an honest-to-God album, *Sleepy Man Blues*.

After joining Jim Kweskin's Jug Band – a hip and funky ensemble that revisits "good time music" from the 1920s and 30s – Geoff is recording more albums and touring the country, mostly two-week engagements in major cities and college towns, booked by my dad. He lures the sparkling and talented Maria D'Amato away from the Even Dozen Jug Band in New York into both his life and the Kweskin ensemble. Soon Geoff and Maria and Louise and I become a tight foursome, getting together several times a week for meals, concerts and listening sessions. Both couples marry in 1964, a few months after my twentieth birthday.

We are seekers. We search for a musical life that rings true, that cuts to the bone. In this, we are part of a movement, perhaps even a cult. I buy in wholeheartedly. Compared to New York, the Cambridge-Boston scene is small and insular. We like to think of ourselves as more real, less show biz. And – Joan Baez notwithstanding – we certainly have fewer opportunities to be "discovered," in the sense of Bob Dylan's or Bill Cosby's rapid rise from Greenwich Village coffeehouses to national renown.

Our world instead revolves around a cauldron of great music parties, constantly simmering. There's one tonight at Bob and Betsy Siggins's place, over on Mount Auburn Street. If Geoff and Maria are the "it" couple of the blues clique, Bob and Betsy hold down a similar spot in its bluegrass/country counterpart. Cambridge is not that big a town and traditional music not that big a scene, but advocates and acolytes somehow find room in both for cliques, squabbles, turf battles. It's all friendly enough, until it isn't.

That's the choice that confronts me as I enter the front door, hang up my winter coat, and stamp the snow from my boots. In the living room, Jim Rooney, a charter member of the Siggins faction, is making the case for Hank Williams versus Jimmie Rodgers, the singing brakeman from Meridian, Mississippi. Both artists get points for short tragic lives, and both are seminal figures in country music. Neither has anything to do with bluegrass, but that distinction doesn't hold water with this group, which feels that any country or mountain song is really a bluegrass song trying to emerge. The arguments can get intense with intellectual firepower – Siggins is studying for his PhD in a career that will eventually take him to a major position at Scripps Research in La Jolla, a long way from his Nebraska roots. And Rooney, from nearby Dedham, is a classics major doing graduate studies in Greek. Over in the corner, Joe Val is quiet, choosing not to take sides. Joe keeps the candle burning for Bill Monroe as the true bluegrass lodestar, and he's reluctant to stray too far from that course. His academic résumé is not Ivy League – he was repairing typewriters, including for Folklore Productions, until he drifted into our music scene. But he possesses true bluegrass bona fides, including a chilling high lonesome tenor voice, and the academic heavyweights defer to him.

In the bedroom, the blues contingent holds forth. That's

where I find Geoff and Maria and Jim Kweskin. Although Jim has been known to pull a fast one by playing an early Gene Autry record, which everybody assumes is Jimmie Rodgers – young Autry sounds just like him – Jim's musical home is blues and its offshoots: jug band music and early jazz. Geoff is 100% blues all the way, won't abide any country or bluegrass. But Maria, who plays old-time fiddle and has traveled south to meet Doc Watson, has been working on him, thinks he may come around eventually. I hope so. Given the range of my earlier role models – from Lightnin' Hopkins to Pete Seeger to Merle Travis to Reverend Gary Davis – I'm drawn to both camps.

Geoff can listen to blues and jug band music all night long. He's loyal to that world and I'm loyal to him. But tonight his ear is drawn to the Jimmie Rodgers record that Bob Siggins is playing in the living room. A look of surprised comprehension passes over his face. He hesitates. And then he actually leaves the blues bedroom in search of that quirky Blue Yodel that Jimmie Rodgers is sending out from the turntable. Maria winks at me and gives a thumbs-up. She has scored a rare victory in the whose-musical-taste-is-hippest sweepstake.

Later, as the party is breaking up, I encounter Dave Wilson, whose *Broadside* periodical chronicles our musical world, deep in conversation with one of his writers, aspiring producer Joe Boyd. They are parsing feedback from Joe's recent article distinguishing the roots-based (and hence more genuine) Cambridge-Boston scene from its more commercial counterpart in New York. It's a long-running dispute.

For us musical pilgrims, the search for the real stuff continues unabated. Easter brings a mammoth gospel show to the Boston Arena, and we watch Claude Jeter and Paul Owens of the Swan Silvertones trade lead vocals on "Mary Don't You Weep." They fling the single microphone back and forth between them, even as they fall to their knees in a choreographed version of the rapture that I observed, years earlier, at the Sister Rosetta Tharpe concert.

The Paul Butterfield Blues Band swaggers into town regularly, performing either at the 47 or at the Unicorn, across the river in Boston. These are another group of seekers, ones who have mastered the street-tough language of Chicago blues. Although happy to hang with the Cambridge crowd, the Butterfield gang seems a bit condescending towards our acoustic music and our less in-your-face vocabulary. I'm taken aback when I see Paul strutting down Putnam Avenue, openly smoking a joint, flaunting his illegal, culture-defining habit. My friends and I smoke plenty of reefer, but it's a hidden pleasure. I'm not ready to defy the authorities – not only the law, but my watchful mother – so overtly.

Before being accepted at Harvard, I was rejected by University of Chicago. It was my first choice, mostly because of the blues scene surrounding the campus. I imagined myself going to South Side blues clubs, learning from those masters. Digging Butterfield's powerful music, I wonder what sort of life that would have offered, what sort of pilgrim I might have become there.

One afternoon, Geoff and I find ourselves at the Unicorn as the Butterfield band is rehearsing and sound checking for the evening gig. Guitarist Michael Bloomfield is teaching the band his arrangement of "Walkin' Blues." Michael is a brilliant blues player; I learn something every time I hear him, which is probably why I'm eager to spend time at his sound check, a generally boring and predictable ritual. But this time things are different; the band is in full creative gear. Paul, although the unchallenged leader, is content to defer to Michael, let him take charge for this arrangement. And it's a beautiful arrangement, fully informed by Robert Johnson's delta original – again, that old recording by a blues master – but at the same time, proudly and immediately of the present moment. It has a strong backbeat; you can dance to it. Michael has the tune figured out, every measure from start to finish. There are passages where he insists on a precise reiteration of a riff, and other passages that are reserved for improvisation.

When the band takes a break, Bloomfield comes over to chat, and I mention that *Revolver*, the brand new Beatles album, contains rhythm-and-blues horns on "I Want To Tell You." Michael can't wait, runs down the street to buy it from the nearest record store. He puts it on the house turntable and, breaking into a childlike grin that covers his entire face, immediately focuses on George Harrison's guitar solo, which I had barely noticed, it's such a small part of the arrangement. But to Bloomfield it is crucial and beautiful, and he's right. It's a sign that I have more lessons to learn, perhaps more mentors to cultivate.

Meanwhile, loud angry voices emanate from the back office. Geoff has been having an argument with George Popodopoulos, the owner. Harsh words are exchanged, some in Greek, Popodopoulos's native language. My Greek is non-existent, but Geoff has learned a few choice curses from Byron Linardos, who has moved from managing the Unicorn to managing the 47. Maybe something about the guy's mother. Whatever the offense, Geoff is summarily booted out of the Unicorn.

*Von Schmidts, Greenhills and Muldaurs listen to the Paul Butterfield Blues Band at the Newport Folk Festival*

I don't want to leave, but I accompany Geoff to the Polish-American Club, where he binds his wounds with alcohol. At the Polish-American Club, Geoff can drink until 1AM on Sunday morning, an hour after the state's strict closing times. Hence his recent burst of ethnic pride. At the bar, I calm him down with talk of baseball, my forte, an area where I'm the leader. The club is intensely proud of Carl Yastrzemski, who eventually is inducted into the National Polish-American Hall of Fame, after leading the Red Sox to the 1967 World Series. Geoff and I spend many hours following Yaz and the Red Sox at Fenway Park and, in winter, Bill Russell's Celtics at Boston Garden. One night, during basketball season, we're listening to an important playoff game on the car radio when we realize that we are just blocks from the Garden. We double-park the car, walk through the unguarded entry, and reach the arena in time to see Russell jam home the winning basket.

Geoff's career advances as the Jug Band continues to tour and to record. When an interviewer from *Time* magazine asks why does the band play "good time music," Geoff quips, "Well, if we lived in good times, maybe we'd play hard time music." Mainstream success, however unlikely last year, now seems within reach. When they appear on the Tonight Show, playing their funky homemade music for millions of people, Jim Kweskin is now king of the local hill, with Geoff his Polish prince. Without noticing or choosing, I seem to have morphed from Geoff's protégé to his courtier, picking him up at the airport, listening to his beefs about the band and taking his side. I'm proud of my famous friend, but also a bit jealous and not fully comfortable with my new role. And the band is changing. Crucially, Mel Lyman joins on harmonica and becomes something of a spiritual leader, especially to Jim. Mel has a way of carrying himself above the fray, as if privy to secrets that only he can access.

As summer 1965 approaches, attention turns again to the Newport Folk Festival. The festival has evolved since Joan Baez soared to prominence in 1959. Pete Seeger presides as a fatherly figure,

*Skip James's first notes at Newport*

an elder statesman leading the crowd in song. Dylan has cemented his position at the front of the artistic parade, mobbed when he ventures into the crowd. His songs have changed – he seems less interested in the broad political struggles that still roil America, like civil rights and the war in Vietnam, and instead focuses on internal, personal issues. Less "Talkin' John Birch Society Blues" and more "It Ain't Me Babe." And closer to home – closer to my home, at any rate – the Kweskin Jug Band has become a crowd favorite.

My dad is an adviser to the festival's Board of Directors, which gives me access not only to a good seat, but to a broad swath of the backstage scene as well. Pete Seeger prepares for his set with a series of stretches. He lies on his back, seemingly exhausted, nearly asleep. Then goes on stage to give an electrifying performance.

The year that the Freedom Singers close the festival alongside Pete, Dylan, Joan and Peter Paul & Mary in the civil rights anthem,

Dear John Fahey,

    Thank you for finding Booker White and bringing him from Mississippi to the Newport Folk Festival. Later, when he played Club 47, I got to hang out with him a bit. A younger man than Skip James, Son House, or Mississippi John Hurt, his energy on "Fixin' To Die" belied the song's subject matter. Booker tore up the 47.

    You, on the other hand, played Club 47 as a none-too-sober afterthought. It seemed like you didn't really want to be there and pretty much phoned in your performance. I was disappointed.

    It wasn't until many years later, after my father died and I took over administering your publishing catalogue, that we connected as people. I came to see you as a sweet, quirky and conflicted soul, and came to hear the layers and strength in your music. The night before your open-heart surgery, you called to make your wishes known, "just in case." When you didn't survive the operation, "just in case" became "right now." Since then I've tried to follow your guidance, including regarding Melody Fahey, and to do right by the songs. I wonder how you would have felt to hear your music used to sell Chevrolets. That was a good year for the songs, and helped Melody fix up the house.

    You are gone, but the John Fahey Trust endures.

My "Dear John" letter

John Fahey, self-portrait

"We Shall Overcome" I'm convinced. We shall overcome; it's only a matter of time and perseverance.

Much of our cult – Geoff, Maria, Louise, von Schmidt and I – is in the crowd on a misty morning when that mysterious blues master Skip James appears. We have been waiting for him so long– at least since Geoff and I fought over his melody – that his entry seems a further validation that the world is changing for the better. Skip joins Booker White, Son House, and the deeply kind Mississippi John Hurt as yet another musical hero who has alchemized from the grooves of old recordings into a flesh-and-blood human being. We have been listening to their recordings for years, straining to understand the words and cop the guitar licks. Now here they are, a pantheon in the flesh. There may be a war in Vietnam, racial injustice may hold sway in much of society, but here in our corner of New England elderly blues giants have come, like gods from on high, to show us a better way.

On the last night of the 1965 festival, something feels different. I'm hanging out backstage as usual, drinking a soda and munching on soggy potato chips, when all of a sudden I'm hustled out of the tent and back into the audience. I've been suddenly cut out of that sanctuary and thrust back into the sea of faces that are about to witness Bob Dylan shake up the musical world by "going electric." As has been well documented, Bob – backed by Michael Bloomfield and other members of the Butterfield Band – turns Newport on its collective ear, with much of American culture to follow. Butterfield himself does not participate, but his swagger infuses the era-changing set.

I don't have much to add to the many reports of that night, except that to me and the rest of our gang, this is not a big surprise. Bob's recording of "Like a Rolling Stone" has been on the radio all summer, and we have been digging the Butterfield gang at Newport. And didn't Howlin' Wolf – a more transgressive and dangerous presence, albeit one not as beloved by the crowd, not seen as one of their own – perform on this very stage, just the night before? Of course Dylan is going to go electric. The question is, how will it sound? Pretty muddy, I'm afraid.

But Dylan's set certainly does warrant its reputation as a divisive milestone. The crowd's booing, Peter Yarrow's nervous attempts to mediate this culture clash, and the general sense of unease all indicate that the times are indeed a-changin'. When Bob returns to the stage, a borrowed acoustic guitar in hand, he sings "It's all over now, Baby Blue."

And for many of us, me included, it is. I'm no longer certain that we shall overcome politically. And culturally, I'm no longer sure that a rediscovered generation of elderly blues masters provides a strong enough tool to unearth America's lost soul. Doubts have begun to creep in.

As the disoriented crowd leaves the Newport concert field, covering their eyes from the suddenly intense house lights on the stadium stanchions, three figures walk to a microphone at the side of the stage that Bob Dylan has recently abandoned. Pete Seeger's long-neck banjo and Jim Kweskin's dreadnought guitar accompany Mel Lyman as he puts his harmonica to his lips and plays a hymn. It feels like a healing balm, perhaps a prayer for the turbulent times to come. Tensions relax, at least for the present moment, as

*Jim Kweskin Jug Band at Newport. Mel Lyman, Maria Muldaur, Geoff Muldaur, Jim Kweskin, Bill Keith. Fritz Richmond not visible*

several thousand people grab their blankets and coolers, and, deep in thought, trudge to their cars.

Geoff is dispirited. Perhaps he senses that the Jug Band's buoyant run is beginning to founder. Their set, preceding Dylan's, was probably the weakest of their Newport efforts over the years. Atypically, the Jug Band seemed to fumble and stumble through a repertoire that they had played perhaps once or twice too often. In contrast to the power of the electric music, the Jug Band more or less squandered a coveted evening slot on the main stage. And Geoff can feel Lyman's growing influence on Kweskin, who is getting ready to dissolve his Jug Band and move to the Lyman Family's commune.

In the next decade, Geoff will join Paul Butterfield's next band, Better Days, and the two of them will swap and combine their distinctive strands of charisma and talent. A few years later, Michael Bloomfield will die of a drug overdose, with Paul to reach a similar end shortly thereafter.

An epilogue: the 1966 Newport Folk Festival is happy to leave 1965 in the rear-view mirror. Dylan is no longer on the bill. Instead, Arlo Guthrie is moving to take Bob's place as his father Woody Guthrie's heir. He regales the crowd with the epic "Alice's Restaurant," which manages to debunk the Vietnam War and the older generation not with direct challenge, but with a series of absurd juxtapositions – like the idea that a citation for littering makes one ineligible to kill in Vietnam.

But for me, the crucial moment comes on the Sunday afternoon "New Folks" concert, where I have been booked for my own ten-minute set. Host Peter Yarrow is a ball of nervous energy, but I'm determined not to get rattled. Joined by my piano-playing partner Jeff Gutcheon, and Geoff Muldaur and Fritz Richmond from the Jug Band, I play instrumentals from my new album *Shepherd of the Highways*. As we send the music out over the afternoon crowd, I feel peaceful and connected. I'm relaxing into the music, inviting the audience to come to me, rather than

*Playing with Jeff Gutcheon*

reaching out to corral them. I feel that I'm using all of my musical lessons while at the same time letting them go. They have become part of me. It's another graduation day, and when I leave the stage, I feel very much in the herd.

And then Rosalie Sorrels, the next artist on the bill, asks me to accompany her. At this point, she's recently left her marriage and her home in Salt Lake City, and is just setting out on the life of a traveling musician. She wants to expand her repertoire and audience beyond folksongs of Idaho and Utah. Rosalie's set also goes well, and then she and I travel to Vermont where, in a living room around a single microphone, we record her album *If I Could Be the Rain*. It's the start of something new for her, and, in a sense, the beginning of a new chapter in my life.

At the Vermont sessions, I'm making my own way, without checking in to see if anyone approves my musical choices. Or maybe I do check with Geoff internally – what would he say? But I'm on my own now.

Driving home after the Newport performances and the recording session in Vermont, my mind goes back to hanging out with Geoff on Martha's Vineyard. Especially watching the sunset from Gay Head, at the island's westernmost edge while a substantial dose of LSD courses through my system. It's the first time this east coast boy sees the sun set into the ocean. The sun's rays pulse off the gentle waves, then through them, and I feel that I've come to an acid-prompted understanding of – well, of everything, it seems. I can almost see the electrons flowing between distinct objects, including myself. (Or is that a swarm of mosquitoes?) Geoff, sitting next to me as we watch the Gay Head clay tumble down the cliff into infinity, is my guide on this trip, and a buddy. Here he is warm and nurturing, my friend who has taught me so much.

The local Wampanoag Indians call this place Aquinnah. They believe that the giant Moshup created the island, including these cliffs, whose distinctive red and black hues were formed when Moshup hurled a whale against the shore. He seems to be tossing me around, as well.

*Playing with Rosalie Sorrels, a few years later*

On the drive down-island from where Moshup's creation was forged, I lean into the soft wooded hills as Geoff's VW van scampers over them, more like a goat than like a machine. This vehicle, and the others that we pass, become a gentle flock of creatures, and I become their shepherd – The Shepherd of the Highways. In the rest of my time in Massachusetts, the sobriquet stays with me, becomes part of my identity, my own creation myth, tossed like that whale towards other rocky shores ahead.

*Revisiting Gay Head (Aquinnah) 2016*

*Site of Moshup's creation*

## 20 YEARS OLD
*Recording with Sam Charters*

In 1964, a year before Dylan's electric transgression, I record my first album, the acoustic *Pickin' the City Blues*, for Prestige Records. I have watched enviously as my friends – Geoff Muldaur, Tom Rush, Jim Kweskin, Bill Keith & Jim Rooney, the Charles River Valley Boys, as well as Jackie Washington – become recording artists. And I wonder when my turn will come?

I see an opening when Sam Charters comes to town. I know his work well, both as the author of *The Country Blues* and as the guy who lugged a reel-to-reel tape recorder to remote Andros Island, where he recorded the wonderful guitarist Joseph Spence and other Bahaman musicians. And he's a player himself, on jug with Dave Van Ronk's Ragtime Jug Stompers, and on piano in a duo with guitarist Danny Kalb.

Sam now runs the folk music division at Prestige Records (Paul Rothchild having moved over to Elektra, where he will produce first the Paul Butterfield Blues Band and then The Doors.) Sam's arrival coincides with my solo

*Sam Charters, Danny Kalb, Dave Van Ronk*

booking at Cholmondeley's (pronounced "Chumley's"), the coffeehouse at Brandeis University. Whether by happenstance or by design, he catches my set, and I fortunately am in good form that night. My singing is true, my guitar licks make sense, and I even manage to engage the friendly audience with jokes and whimsy.

To seal the deal, I invite Sam and his wife, the author Ann Charters, whose specialty is the Beat writers, to spend the night at my Cambridge apartment. I give them the bed, and sleep on my couch.

Sam and Ann and I get along, and I get the impression that he sees me as a viable part of the Cambridge folk scene. That's part of his mission at Prestige, to represent the growing folk music communities by putting their music on vinyl. Some months later, I join him in New York, where he's producing my first album and I'm sleeping on his couch. I bring along Geoff Muldaur and ask Bill Lee to play bass. Bill, an opera composer, has been the go-to bass player in the New York scene, including for Odetta, which is how we become acquainted. His precocious son Spike is, at this point, in kindergarten and not yet making movies. Bill and I rehearse at Izzy Young's Folklore Center, a central hotspot on MacDougal Street. Maybe I ask Izzy beforehand, or maybe I just assume it will be OK; the Folklore Center is that kind of place.

> *In the summer of 1969, Izzy Young has moved the Folklore Center a few blocks east, to Sixth Avenue, over the Waverly Theater. He presents me there in concert, which why I'm not at the Woodstock Music Festival that same weekend, up the road apiece.*
>
> *A few years later we interact in a different setting, the Sweets Mill Music Camp, high (in several senses) in the Sierras. There, skinny-dipping and discovering psychedelics, Izzy transforms from "Izzy from New York" to "Izzy from the Universe."*
>
> *Eventually he becomes "Izzy from Stockholm," where the Folklore Center finds its final home.*

Although I've recorded in living rooms, this is my first time in a professional recording studio, with high-end microphones and a control booth and headphones. I'm too inexperienced to be very nervous. I forego the headphones and listen to the three of us play, as if we're on some coffeehouse stage. I include songs learned from Pete Seeger and Willie Dixon, as well as a few of my own compositions. The album is released in March 1965.

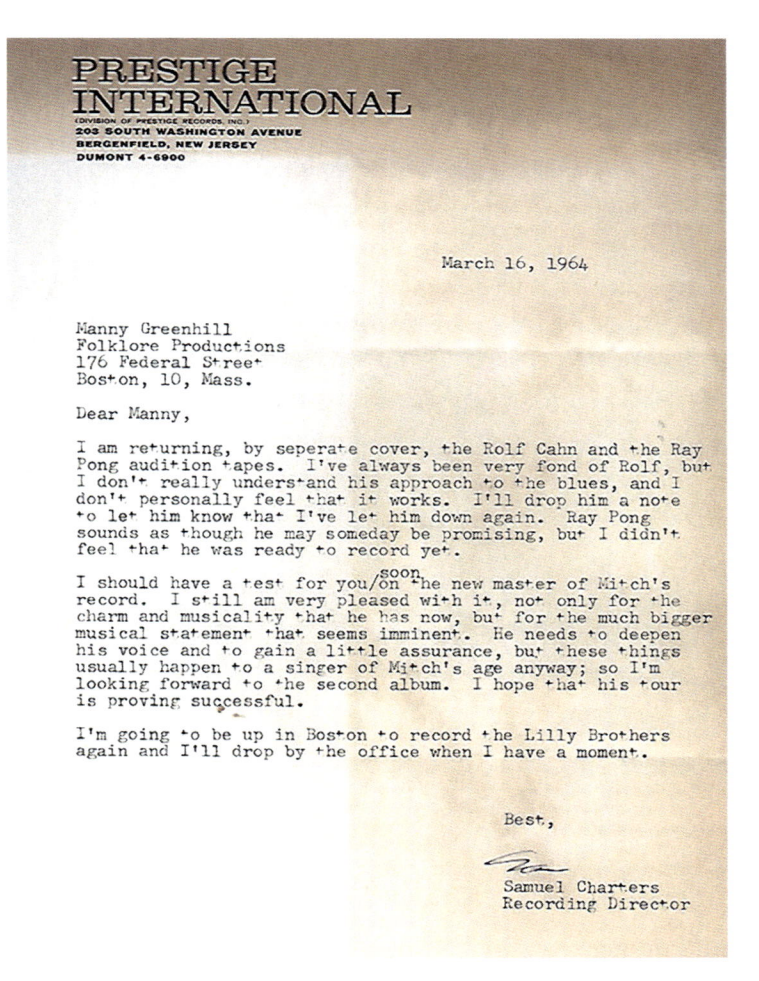

> **PRESTIGE INTERNATIONAL**
> (DIVISION OF PRESTIGE RECORDS, INC.)
> 203 SOUTH WASHINGTON AVENUE
> BERGENFIELD, NEW JERSEY
> DUMONT 4-6900
>
> March 16, 1964
>
> Manny Greenhill
> Folklore Productions
> 176 Federal Street
> Boston, 10, Mass.
>
> Dear Manny,
>
> I am returning, by seperate cover, the Rolf Cahn and the Ray Pong audition tapes. I've always been very fond of Rolf, but I don't really understand his approach to the blues, and I don't personally feel that it works. I'll drop him a note to let him know that I've let him down again. Ray Pong sounds as though he may someday be promising, but I didn't feel that he was ready to record yet.
>
> I should have a test for you/on soon the new master of Mitch's record. I still am very pleased with it, not only for the charm and musicality that he has now, but for the much bigger musical statement that seems imminent. He needs to deepen his voice and to gain a little assurance, but these things usually happen to a singer of Mitch's age anyway; so I'm looking forward to the second album. I hope that his tour is proving successful.
>
> I'm going to be up in Boston to record the Lilly Brothers again and I'll drop by the office when I have a moment.
>
> Best,
>
> Samuel Charters
> Recording Director

*Sam to Manny, judgement day*

In 1966 I record a second album for Prestige. This time all tunes are instrumental, and Fritz Richmond plays bass, along with Muldaur and Jeff Gutcheon, the stride piano player with whom I have been developing a duo. Jeff, Fritz and I bunk in at John Sebastian's apartment. John is out of town, but his girlfriend welcomes us, although in the middle of the night John calls and they have a big fight. The album is released as *Shepherd of the Highway*, with a cover painted by Eric von Schmidt.

Sam's jazz experience is helpful at this stage of my development. Muldaur, Gutcheon and I have taken to re-harmonizing tunes, putting new – to our minds, hipper – chords to old melodies. We get a kick out of modulating to a different key, but doing so in a seamless, almost sneaky way. Sam tolerates this up to a point, but won't let us go too far. You don't just drop chords into tunes, he admonishes. Chords have to come organically from the melodies.

As the years go on, Sam Charters and I maintain our relationship, largely through Dave Van Ronk. When not producing the likes of Country Joe and the Fish, Sam is Dave's occasional record producer; and I become Dave's manager. After colon cancer fells Dave – and despite his best efforts, he is unable to avoid the priest who scurries into his hospital room for last rites, even as those of us close to the patient are shooed away – Sam and I make one last deal. We are each obeying nature's call in adjacent urinals at Dave's memorial service, in Judson Memorial Church, when Sam agrees to give Dave's final recordings to Andrea, his widow. We wash our hands before shaking.

# WANDERLUST
## *Target Practice with Hunter Thompson*

Ever since I aimed the family DeSoto out into East 21st Street as a five-year-old, I've felt the call of the open road. It seems so romantic to leave familiar streets behind and strike out into unknown territory. Necessity meets romance when I begin courting Louise Rice. We meet in suburban Brookline, just outside Boston, where her family maintains a boardinghouse. But she lives in the family's other home, a wooden two-story house in Daytona Beach, Florida.

When Louise and I begin our courtship, she is still a senior at Seabreeze High School, while I am a college freshman. Hitchhiking is my usual mode of long-distance travel, and the trips are often challenging. I stick out my thumb in northern Virginia, just south of D.C., and am picked up by a beefy guy in a big car. He says that he will take me to Danville, but when he turns off the main road and drives into a stretch of isolated woods, I know this is not the way. I ask where are we going, and he makes some vague reply, there's something he needs to do. As the woods become deeper and the road grows more empty and isolated, I grow concerned, frightened. I remember my pocketknife and draw it from my jeans. Trying to seem relaxed and nonchalant – no big deal, this happens every day –, I open the blade and use it to clean my fingernails.

With a jolt, the driver turns the car around and returns to the main road. He makes some excuse and leaves me there – no closer to Danville, but safe and in one piece.

I grab a long ride with a trucker, going all the way to Georgia. I crawl into the bunk behind the cab seats and fall asleep. I awake to a humid night in South Carolina, sounds of crickets and semi-tandems. The truck has stopped and the driver is gone. I climb out of the cab and stretch my legs. It looks like a truck stop, but before I can explore, he returns and we are on the road again. He seems in much better spirits, I guess because, as he eventually lets on, the truck stop doubles as a brothel.

A bearded, long-haired young man with a guitar is suspect when he sticks out his thumb by a highway outside of Savannah. That's one ride that never materializes, so I eventually go to the bus station, where border patrol officers suspect that I'm a Cuban revolutionary, sneaking in to overthrow the capitalist system.

Eventually I reach north Florida and Louise. And her beloved horses, Hoppy and Happy. Although I'm a totally inexperienced rider, I want to impress Louise, so I attempt to ride bareback, as she does. No saddle for Cowboy Mitch – a blanket and bridle is all I need. My thighs strain to accommodate Hoppy's broad sweaty back. I kick her in the gut, and off we go. At first the big horse lumbers along the familiar trail, bored and nonchalant. But soon she gets the idea that I'm a lot smaller than she and don't have a clue. I'm trying to coax her into a relaxed loping canter, when suddenly she takes off. She ignores my feeble commands and bolts away, tearing through the flat woodland, straight towards a busy highway. I'm hanging on to her mane, afraid of her speed and power, but more afraid that I will be responsible for killing or maiming the horse and that will be the end of my romance with Louise. But somehow we cross the road safely and continue through the piney woods until Hoppy comes to a sudden halt. She pitches me forward, over her head and onto the sandy soil. Once she has thrown me, the horse feels content and stops to paw the earth and chew some grass. Louise, once she catches up, seems equally concerned with my health and welfare as with Hoppy's. That's sweet, surprising, and perhaps telling.

Travel becomes easier when I acquire my own vehicle. The first is Maggie Monstercar, an Oldsmobile that I buy second-hand in Boston, in preparation for my first trip west, in the summer of 1964. I have taken a semester's sabbatical from college and have persuaded my dad to book a modest tour. The itinerary includes a gig in Salt Lake City, where I first meet and share a stage with Rosalie Sorrels, the start of a long musical and personal relationship. After the concert she throws an epic party at the "big fine house" she will later evoke in her song "Travelin' Lady." (Six years later, my band The Frontier will accompany her on an album of the same name.)

The party is rich in food, particularly a green chili dish that is a specialty of the house. And rich too in musicians, including a baby-faced songwriter, just out of the armed forces, named Bruce Phillips. He sings a few new compositions, including "If I Could Be the Rain." It will be some years before he reinvents himself as U Utah Phillips, the Golden Voice of the Great Southwest. But the inspiration and the talent are already in place.

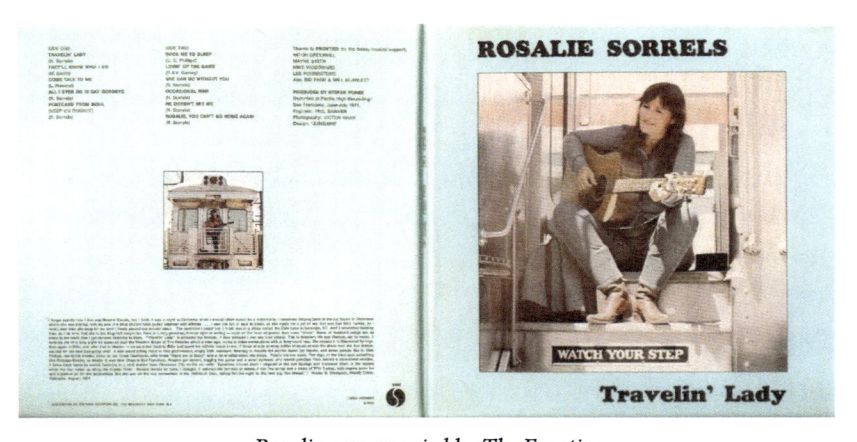

*Rosalie accompanied by The Frontier*

In Ketchum, Idaho, I perform in the pulpit of the church where Rosalie's grandfather once preached. It's now a bar, and one of the patrons is a shy *Wall Street Journal* stringer named Hunter Thompson. He is researching a story on Hemingway. Hunter writes that he's not surprised that Hemingway killed himself, but is curious why he chose Ketchum as the setting. Decades later, Hunter will end his own life in a similar way, a rifle shot to the head.

Later on the trip, I visit Hunter's home in the Valley of the Moon in Northern California, where he is working on his book about the Hells Angels. Surprised and a bit scandalized that I have never fired a gun, he decides to teach me the basics. The first gun in my hand is a .44 magnum, the type of powerful weapon (I later learn) that can penetrate an engine block. (And Hunter, frustrated at a car that leaves him stranded on a freeway, eventually uses it for just that purpose.)

The gun is heavier than I've come to expect from watching horseback shootouts in the movies. Hunter has me aim at a target painted on a trashcan, but gives little guidance beyond that. I steady my hand, as best I can, draw a bead on the target, and pull the trigger. Then, immediately, all goes black. "Not bad," I hear Hunter say encouragingly. But I can't see a thing – the powerful recoil has plunged the heavy metal into my forehead, and blood now streams over my eyes. An early lesson from Hunter: take dead aim at your target and live with the gory consequences.

Naked except for the gun, he hunts a deer. His wife Sandy cooks it with honey. Their son Juan, who will eventually discover his father's body, is a toddler.

My first glimpse of the Pacific Ocean is at Tomales Bay, north of San Francisco. I've been imagining it for so long! Excited, I scramble down a steep bank – steeper than it looks at first glance – and splash in the water, like a child. Somewhere a seal barks. Out beyond the waves, an otter swims on its back while dining

January 30, 1970
Woody Creek, CO

Dear Mitch

God only knows where you are, so I'll send one copy of this to the old Mi-Wuk Village address, and another c/o the record co. I was trying to get control of my desk last night & I found an old letter from you   talking mainly about the Detroit Lions. I guess I was two years early; next year they'll mop up in the Central. Take my word for it...

As for me, I plan to take whatever small profits I get off this new book and set up a mescaline factory in Woody Creek. Hopefully I can make enough on sales to pay the rent and keep myself in a blazing stupor for the rest of my days. I bought a set of $100 earphones with red lights that flash at 95 decibels. I've worn out two copies of Memphis Underground & burned 2 cords of pinion wood this winter... get naked & gobble mescaline by a huge fire & the whole house vibrating with sound. Try it sometime; it's fun.

Ciao

Hunter
& Hello to Louise

*Hunter makes plans*

on abalone. This is a different kind of nature from severe New England, wilder in some ways, more benign in others.

In Berkeley a few nights later, after performing at the Cabal, I see that deer have come down from the Berkeley Hills to graze on the grounds of the University of California; we have none in Harvard Yard.

I continue south and stay with Hunter again, this time at a cabin in Big Sur. We are high above the Pacific Ocean, and the sun sets into it every night. Now the deer come right up to the porch, as the fog licks their hooves. We are still eating venison that Sandy brought from home, so these deer are safe from Hunter's arsenal.

One of Hunter's writing buddies has joined us, and he agrees to put me up at his place in Topanga Canyon, while I perform at the Ash Grove in Los Angeles. I share a dressing room with the intimidating Big Mama Thornton, who first recorded "Hound Dog." She is a powerful presence and a woman of great warmth and big gripes.

*You ain't nothin' but a hound dog, been snoopin' round the door*
*You can wag your tail, but I ain't gonna feed you no more*

At one point during the engagement, a precocious high school student named Ry Cooder drops by to check out the music, soak up any licks that he may find useful, and say hello. Sixteen years later we will work together on Walter Hill's film *The Long Riders*. I play the singer and guitarist in a brothel frequented by Jesse James and his cohorts. At one point Walter Hill stops to listen as my band mates and I are passing the time by swapping tunes. He says wistfully, "You know, if I want to jam, to try something out, I first need to talk somebody into giving me six million dollars."

After the Ash Grove, I head back east. Maggie Monstercar gobbles up the southwest desert. A summer thunderstorm sends water pinging off the hood. I play a few nights in Santa Fe. Louise and I talk on the phone, and this is where we agree to marry, later that summer.

The Oldsmobile returns me to Cambridge. When a highway patrol officer stops me, just south of the George Washington Bridge, I've been driving for two days. I'm a bundle of nerves. Fortunately he doesn't find the tabs of peyote in the trunk, a present for the bride-to-be.

A couple of vehicles later, I acquire a Volkswagen van. Geoff Muldaur and I take it out to Fritz Richmond's parents' place, in suburban Newton. That handyman wizard, who plays jug and washtub bass with Geoff in Jim Kweskin's Jug Band, builds a double bed into it. My journeys take on a new rhythm, and travel becomes less challenging.

Geoff and Maria and Louise and I rent a place in Sarasota, close to Eric von Schmidt and his friends in the art world. Pelicans swoop down from the sky, then soar up again, their deep beaks filled with meals for their nestlings. Ramblin' Jack Elliott shows up, resuming the long-running story that began – or probably continued from his previous stop – back on Huntoon Street, some years ago. Eric is working on a series of paintings about the American West, large canvases of rifle smoke and bloody arrows.

Louise and I drive farther south and explore the Everglades. My two-week engagement at the Gaslight in Coconut Beach, south of Miami, becomes a longer stay, and we become part of another local music scene, not all that different from Club 47's. After the Gaslight has closed for the night, we continue the music

*Joseph Spence, a unique take on guitar*

in a compound of small cottages beneath royal palms. Many a sunrise finds us still playing, singing and talking. On my twenty-second birthday, I dance on a narrow mantle above a fireplace. Louise is four months pregnant.

Eager to meet Joseph Spence, the great Bahaman guitarist, I somehow secure a gig with Nassau's only folk music club. It turns out to be a white enclave, not really what I was looking for. But I do develop a relationship with Spence. On the afternoon of my concert I lose control of the motor scooter that I've borrowed. It and I are both scratched and bruised, but the concert proceeds and the white folks are suitably entertained.

Some months later Joseph stays with Louise and me when he tours the States, including a gig at Club 47. It is perhaps his first time in a big American city, and I am concerned when he disappears for the entire day. Has something happened to him? Is he lost? How will he find his way? I'm nervously pacing outside Club 47, when Joseph strolls up, guitar in hand. He has been exploring the town on foot, and is, as usual, fully in control of himself and his place in the world. He takes the stage and begins to play some guitar licks that seem to astonish even himself. He looks down at his fingers in amazement and gives a long, satisfied chuckle.

The next day I drive Joseph to the airport for a flight to Los Angeles. There he will play the Ash Grove while staying with Taj Mahal and Ry Cooder, who have formed a band. I'm beginning to feel antsy, and California is sounding better and better, all the time.

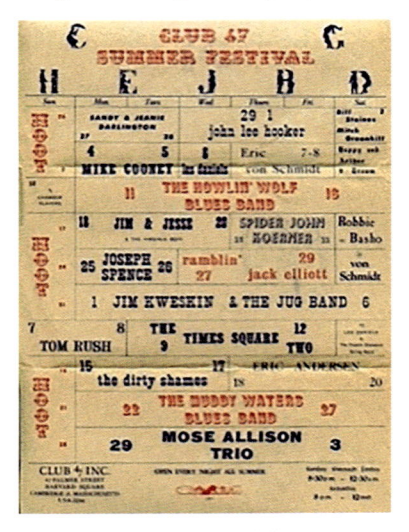

*More music at Club 47*

Friends so now am Hoping to here from you soon so things there are very quiet. so that is good so Fritz and the boys leave town for few weeks so that very good. and you taking things easy. that is alright - so now i would not say much this time but i will close with love to you Your Dearest old Friend my Wife say Best regard to you and Wife

Joseph Spence

so i will like to go to California i have a Brother live there i may come across him he preach.

*from Joseph, 1966*

## 23 YEARS OLD
*On to California*

In 1967 I'm still living on Kinnaird Street in Cambridge, with Louise and a rapidly growing Mattie. The house is a duplex on a rutted street halfway between the high culture of Harvard Square and Central Square's more blue-collar aesthetic. It's a funky structure, with exposed water pipes in the basement that in winter need to be wrapped in blankets so they don't freeze. (I try electric blankets once, then think better of it.) The water heater needs to be lit by hand, and we have to remember to turn it off when we leave, or else the faucets release geysers of steam when we return. But we have five small rooms to live in, one side of a three-story duplex. Next door is a mirror-image residence that houses, at various times, Rick Turner, Mark Spoelstra and Dynamite Annie Johnson, all of whom I will soon re-encounter in California.

Fritz Richmond lives around the corner. Geoff and Maria Muldaur, also new parents, live a bit farther west. Club 47, a short walk away, now presents as much electric fare as it does acoustic folk music, the result of both Dylan's electric turn and the Beatles' growing popularity.

Those Liverpool lads don't sound half bad. In fact, they sound wonderful! Rock seems a lot more vibrant than it did when folk music seduced me, now all of ten years ago.

> Dear Jon Landau,
>
> Thanks for getting us good seats to the Springsteen concert. I hadn't thought that far ahead, when we followed Ron Kovic past your security guards. I figured that the inspiration for "Born On the Fourth of July" would be able to crash the line, especially after Ron popped a wheelie in his wheel chair. But I hadn't realized that we would then be in the bowels of the Sports Arena, without a view of the stage.
>
> Nor, I confess, did I recall that you were my star guitar student, back in Cambridge. I'm glad that you did, and that you somehow recognized me. I flatter myself that some of those songs I taught you, perhaps the Guthrie ones, may have made their way to The Boss.

*My "Dear Jon" letter*

I still perform at Club 47, Cholmondeley's, and a few other venues. But it seems like I have been living in the Cambridge-Boston hothouse scene forever. It is beginning to feel oppressive, especially my father's strong presence in it. When crises arise – like when my friends in the Kweskin Jug Band leave Manny for Albert Grossman's more aggressively commercial approach – I feel squeezed and uncomfortable, my loyalties torn yet again. And I resent that others in my group of players and appreciators don't have this problem; their parents are far away, safely hidden from commentary.

And I have completed my studies at Harvard, so that's no longer holding me. Academia's charm has by now worn off, and by my senior year I manage to avoid taking any classes that require waking up before noon. Jim Field and I, after some debate as to whether we really want to participate in the ritual, eventually don cap and gown, and march through Harvard Yard to receive our diplomas. We are now full-fledged baccalaureate hipsters.

I have fond memories of my trips to California. The lifestyle seems freer there, less confined by tradition and protocol. The weather is definitely more to my liking, as I'm getting tired of shoveling snow and navigating icy roads. I recall picking up Geoff and Maria at the airport, following a Jug Band tour of the west, and marveling at Maria's bronze and beautiful skin, toasted by the California sun.

In the fall of 1967 Geoff Muldaur and I catch one final game at Fenway Park – Yastrzemski obliges with two home runs as the Red Sox shut out the Cardinals in a World Series contest – before I pack up the family and head west. Although I still have many lessons to learn, including from musician mentors, these mentors are no longer familial figures – with, as we shall see, one exception. And though I am still a long ways from mature, I am no longer being raised by musical mavericks. I'm becoming one of them.

A couple of years later, in Northern California's redwood country, I find a different musical community, a raggedy, grassroots collection of city refugees like myself. Mayne Smith, Mark Spoelstra and I form The Frontier. In this country-rock band I learn the pleasures of playing for dancers and finding a common rhythmic bond between the bandstand and the dance floor. We play rooms like Uncle Sam's in Sebastopol, the Freight & Salvage and New Orleans House in Berkeley, and the Inn of the Beginning in Cotati. Like Club 47, these are musical asylums that foster an

*The Frontier – Mayne Smith, Mitch, Lee Poundstone, Michael Woodward and Dave Holt – on stage at Uncle Sam's, Sebastopol, California*

interplay between tradition and innovation, where trying out new ideas, new songs, and new guitar solos is tolerated, even expected. When everything clicks, the energy elevates, the dancers groove, and all seems right with the world.

At some point, maybe it's on the stage at Uncle Sam's, I look across at my sweaty band mates laying down a groove, and out at the dance floor, where shadows are bobbing up and down, and beyond that to the tables where people, some of whose entrance fee was paid in food stamps, are listening in deep concentration.

When it's my turn to take a guitar solo, I step forward on the bandstand and put my fingers on the instrument's neck. It's a Fender Telecaster now, not the Gibson J-45 of my early guitar studies. But I feel the presence of my mentors: Pete Seeger's balance and empathy, Rolf Cahn's theory and practice, Reverend Davis's Saturday night and Sunday morning, Eric von Schmidt's approach to life as one big art project. I experience again the torn loyalties of Merle Travis's lure, Lightnin' Hopkins's strutting pride, Jackie Washington's fraternal protection, Geoff Muldaur's wealth of hipster knowledge.

I close my eyes and put these into my guitar solo. And I feel that I have at last gotten inside the music.

By now the Cambridge-Boston music scene has gradually dispersed, its constituent parts split off like splinters from a log. Some charter members, like Geoff and Maria, are in Woodstock, New York, where Albert Grossman, Bob Dylan, and the Band have established a hip fiefdom. Fritz Richmond lives in Laurel Canyon, in the Hollywood Hills, where he works as a recording engineer. Jim Kweskin and the Lyman Family are in Kansas. Others, like Jack Landrón (as Jackie Washington is now known) and Jeff Gutcheon, my piano-playing music partner, are in New York. Jack has resumed his original goal, acting, which is what he studied at Emerson College. And Gutch continues to develop the stride piano style in which he honors Mattie Greenhill and Jenny Muldaur with ragtime compositions in their names. He eventually helps to develop the hit show *Ain't Misbehavin'* and becomes a quilter of some renown.

In the years to come, I will find other satisfying music scenes, but in retrospect the one I grew up in seems special. It provided two families. One was the household in Dorchester, hosting a series of powerfully talented guests who treat me like a favored nephew. Their avuncular care and instruction has guided me, has provided a towrope for the years to follow.

The other family was the fellowship of musical seekers in and around Cambridge and Boston, who provided an ocean for this fish to swim in. It was an environment that treasured both tradition and originality, so long as each informed the other. It will be years before I realize how rare that is.

In my more mature years, one more musical mentor becomes a virtual family relation – Doc Watson.

# THE VIEW FROM
# DOC WATSON'S FUNERAL

Laurel Springs Baptist Church is packed to the rafters, every seat taken. Downstairs, the area usually used for bake-offs and Sunday school is also full. An audio feed provides sound both down there and outside, where a substantial crowd has gathered on the lawn and in the parking lot. Down the hill, on Route 421, a revolving red light on top of a patrol car flickers in the morning mist, as it cautions oncoming traffic. Above and around us, the hills of western North Carolina provide a respite to the eye, and an invitation to contemplation.

Doc Watson's body lies in an open coffin. He is dressed in his performing clothes: dark slacks and a western-cut shirt, this one sporting a vaguely Southwestern pattern. It's a marked departure from a few decades ago, when the body of Merle Watson, Doc's son and music partner, lay dressed in a tuxedo that he hated and hardly ever wore. A few feet away, in the front row, are Doc's brothers David, who lives nearby, and Linney, who flew in from Oklahoma. Beside them sit Doc's granddaughter Karen and her children. Doc's daughter Nancy and grandson Richard, both battling health problems, visited earlier, before the crowd arrived.

And what a crowd! Some men are dressed in overalls. But many, like me and others whom Doc touched and influenced, now gathering on the dais next to the minister, wear dark suits. The ladies occupy a similar spectrum between work clothes and special clothes. My flight from California was an easy jaunt compared to the two young guitar players who arrived bleary-eyed after a trek from Japan. Others, closer, drove. There are college students, farmers, truck drivers, and guitar aficionados.

I find myself looking at the lifeless body. In my limited experience, I've never felt comfortable in the presence of an open casket. It's not a tradition in the world that I come from, and I generally find that it makes me feel further away from, rather than closer to the dearly departed. I, after all, will walk out of Laurel Springs Baptist Church; Doc, on the other hand, will be carried by pallbearers, including me. After we lay him in the Carolina clay, David Watson will take my hand and assure me, "We'll meet him again."

But now, as I look at his prone remains, encased by flowers and a wooden box, I find myself thinking back to any one of a hundred conversations. I dial the number. He picks up. "How's Doc?" I begin.

"I'll not complain," he responds. "How's Mitchell?" And we're off.

First we talk business – my company, Folklore Productions, has been representing him since 1964, when Ralph Rinzler handed the job over to my father. But eventually the conversation turns to music, or family, or how to wire a house.

It's hard to accept that now those days are gone, that Doc won't be answering the phone. Or telling a story. Or singing about Omie Wise or Milk Cow Blues or Summertime. Or, honor of honors, inviting a guitar solo with those magic words, "Pick it, son."

I first meet Doc at the 1963 Newport Folk Festival. He comes with others, including Tom Ashley (whom Jim Field and I first heard at Galax), Fred Price, and Clint Howard. Doc's wife Rosa Lee sings, as does his mother Annie. Rosa Lee's father Gaither Carlton plays fiddle. It is a portable Watauga County ecosystem, right there amidst the mansions and tennis courts of Newport, Rhode Island. And to me, a northeastern

THE VIEW FROM DOC WATSON'S FUNERAL        157

city boy just entering college, it provides a window into a beautiful world of southern mountain music, deep family ties, and a close relationship with nature.

Later Doc will lament that he can no longer hear the birds and insects of his boyhood, sounds that once guided his sightless wanderings through the Blue Ridge hills of his youth. As the environment has changed, those creatures have left the area. And once he brings me up short by musing, "If my father hadn't bought my uncle's car, I don't know when I'd have ever got to town." Meaning Boone, some ten miles away from the family home in Deep Gap.

A short while after Newport, Doc performs at Club 47. This time there is no Watauga County ecosystem; Doc plays solo. Solo performers are common at the 47, but this is different, a whole other level of connection, commitment and musicianship. When Doc tears into "Black Mountain Rag," I wonder if the plaster will peel off the walls of that venerable room. And when he sings of Tom Dula, it is clear that he feels a personal stake and holds strong opinions on who was to blame for Laurie Foster's murder. He is clearly nourished by some powerful wellspring, even as he eagerly ventures outside its musical boundaries.

Doc soon recruits his son Merle, named after Travis, to play with him. I encounter them in Lenox, that town in western Massachusetts where Pete Seeger agreed to work with Manny. Manny now runs the

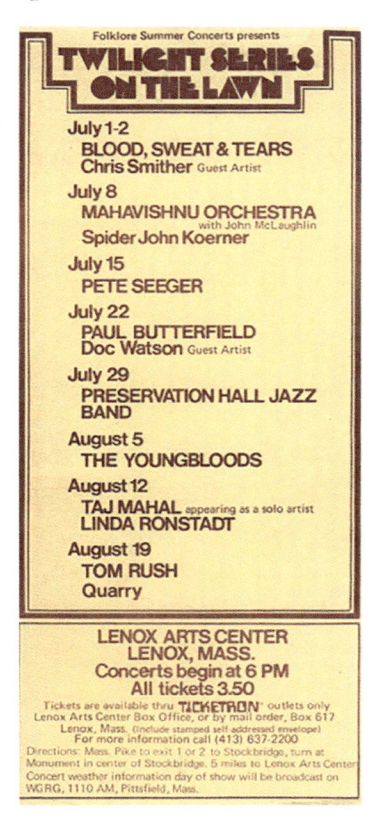

> Folklore Summer Concerts presents
> **TWILIGHT SERIES ON THE LAWN**
>
> July 1-2
> BLOOD, SWEAT & TEARS
> Chris Smither Guest Artist
>
> July 8
> MAHAVISHNU ORCHESTRA
> with John McLaughlin
> Spider John Koerner
>
> July 15
> PETE SEEGER
>
> July 22
> PAUL BUTTERFIELD
> Doc Watson Guest Artist
>
> July 29
> PRESERVATION HALL JAZZ BAND
>
> August 5
> THE YOUNGBLOODS
>
> August 12
> TAJ MAHAL appearing as a solo artist
> LINDA RONSTADT
>
> August 19
> TOM RUSH
> Quarry
>
> LENOX ARTS CENTER
> LENOX, MASS.
> Concerts begin at 6 PM
> All tickets 3.50
> Tickets are available thru TICKETRON outlets only Lenox Arts Center Box Office, or by mail order, Box 617 Lenox, Mass. (include stamped self-addressed envelope) For more information call (413) 637-2200
> Directions: Mass. Pike to exit 1 or 2 to Stockbridge, turn at Monument in center of Stockbridge, 5 miles to Lenox Arts Center Concert weather information day of show will be broadcast on WGRG, 1110 AM, Pittsfield, Mass.

*The lineup at Lenox*

non-classical music series there, and this is where Merle Watson and I begin our friendship. Along with Geoff Muldaur – who is now singing with the headliner, Paul Butterfield – we shoot pool in a wood-paneled room deep in the Berkshire Hills. For some unexplained reason, pre-Columbian art pieces sit on a fireplace mantel. Geoff is the best pool player and pretty much runs the table, while Merle and I get to know each other.

On stage, Doc and Merle work their twin-guitar magic, melodic lines darting between harmony and counterpoint, clean and precise and heart-felt. Ferocious picking is interspersed with ballads that seem as old as dirt.

After I join the family business in California, my relationship with Merle deepens. He asks me to co-produce a series of albums for the Watsons, most of which we mix in Nashville, but some of which we record elsewhere. In Todd, North Carolina, for instance, a short drive from Doc and Merle's homes. There, after one stretch of sessions, Merle and I load the multi-track tape recorder into the back of his van, and drive to Nashville. We want to make sure that our mixes accurately reflect the recording, so the machine goes with the tape. Out of the Blue Ridge we drive, and over the Smokies, down into East Tennessee. By nightfall we are covering the machine with a blanket and carrying the big reels of tape into my Nashville hotel room. As I drift off to sleep, I think of the magnetic particles on that tape, of patterns etched as notes fly off guitars and into microphones. Sound waves, to be sure. But it doesn't take too much imagination to see in those waves the highway from Deep Gap, and the journey that the music has traveled.

As I gain more experience and as my dad ages, I book more gigs for the Watsons and start to take on greater responsibilities in other areas, as well. At one point the Serbian-born master luthier Bozo Podunavac approaches me with an offer to give a twelve-string guitar to Doc. The Watsons play only Gallagher six-strings and have an exclusive arrangement with that Tennessee craftsman. But they have no commitments regarding twelve-string guitars, so I pursue the opportunity further. Soon, however, I find myself out of my depth, as I try to work my way through a thicket of what the "gift" may entail. I find Bozo indirect and hard to read. It all seems murky and full of tacit understandings that are beyond the scope of my limited experience. I'm feeling increasing pressure that I may screw up, may make the Watsons look bad and hurt Bozo's feelings.

Eventually it is Merle who guides me through the negotiations to a conclusion that works for both parties. Doc gets the twelve-string and Bozo gets Doc's seal of approval. I feel relief and appreciate Merle's generous help.

Some twenty years later, after Merle has passed and I am about to observe a birthday well into my middle years, a large package is delivered to the office door. It's either a small coffin or a large guitar. Opening it, I am relieved to find the latter. It is, in fact the same Bozo twelve-string from years past. But now it plays even better than it did originally. Doc has had work done on the action, now low and fast, and on the intonation, now perfect, even high up the neck.

Stunned and puzzled, I call Doc and ask what is this all about.

*The Bozo 12-string. "I wanted to see your face when you opened the case"*

"Well," he chuckles, "I was going to leave it to you in my will. But I wanted to see your face when you opened the case."

And now, many years later – after years of recording sessions, business meetings, and sets at Merlefest, the musical gathering in Merle's honor – I'm a good deal older than the Doc Watson I first met. I've experienced the sad honor of serving as pallbearer at Merle's funeral, as well as at Doc's. My own father has passed, and I run the family business with my son Matt. Family connections run deep between the Watsons and the Greenhills.

Early on, Doc proposed a pact: we would never discuss politics or religion. As a secular Jew, I could see the logic, and I readily agreed. But I guess that I was the first one to break the agreement, when I spent a few minutes trying to convince Doc to vote for John Kerry rather than George Bush. "I'll think on it," he half-snorted, half-chuckled.

Then, a year or so later, it was Doc's turn. He was concerned, not so much with the body politic, but with the prospects for my mortal soul. Hesitantly, as if a bit embarrassed but still believing and determined, Doc ventured that he could not rest easy until he had shown me a path to salvation. He urged me to seriously consider baptism.

I doubt that Doc voted for Kerry, and my soul remains as much at risk as it did on the afternoon of that phone call. But his concern was just the latest of the many deep and important gifts that I received from Doc Watson – as a friend, and also as a role model.

Doc shows me that getting meaning from one's life is more than getting meaning from one's music. His music is embedded in his life, not apart. His is a life in balance and in context.

The phone sits silent on my desk. Doc may no longer be on this line. But his music still resonates, as do his examples of fair and ethical dealings, and fidelity to who he was and where he came from. Maybe, in another world, he again hears the birds and insects of his youth.

Meanwhile I find myself moving towards the pulpit, having been asked to testify, on behalf of my friend and mentor, to those gathered at Laurel Springs Baptist Church. Outside, the Blue Ridge waits in green anticipation to receive its latest noble son. And while I may not be saved – when David Watson tells me that we'll meet Doc again, I can reply only "I hope you're right" – I have been called.

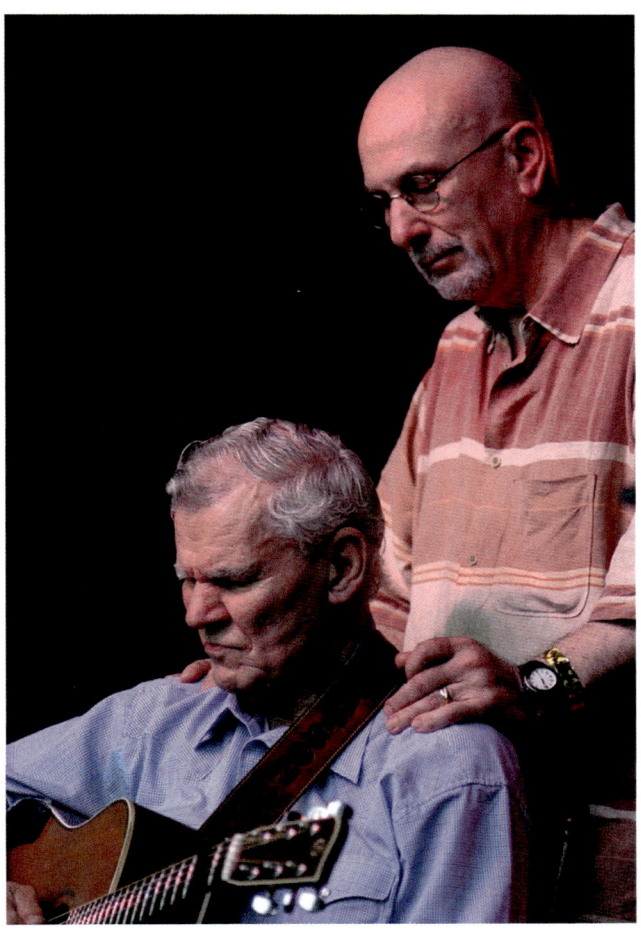

*"Remembering Merle" session at Merlefest*

# THE VIEW FROM MIKE SEEGER'S MEMORIAL

As Pete Seeger unwinds his still lanky frame, we can almost feel his bones creak. At ninety years old, he has come to this suburban community center, on the outskirts of Washington, to say goodbye to his younger brother Mike, and that means leading us in one more song.

I have been Mike's agent for a while, so have been following his decline with concern. The cancer had been with him for some time. The last time we met, after a performance at UCLA, we had to find him some late-night protein as a precaution, and wound up at a decidedly modest diner in West Los Angeles, where Mike downed a midnight breakfast of bacon and eggs.

But I hadn't realized that our most recent conversation, about mundane business matters, would be our last. Shortly thereafter he emailed that he had decided against further treatment, as that was not the kind of life that he wished to prolong. Then came word that friendly musicians were gathering at his rural Virginia home to send him off in style. And then, ominously, word that Mike had sent them away, saying, "I don't want to hear any more music."

Familiar faces populate the memorial gathering. Sister Peggy Seeger plays a banjo tribute. I've been running into her occasionally for decades, including at the folk music gathering that she and her then-husband, the great balladeer Ewan MacColl, hosted in London.

And there is a full contingent of Mike's wives: Alice, Marge and Alexia, all on good terms and on the same page. When I mention this to Marge, she tells me that she and Alice were friends before either of them met Mike, and they weren't about to let him get in the way of that.

Ry Cooder, who just the day before landed in California from a tour of Australia, has packed himself into another transcontinental air trip to pay his respects. Was it only last year that I observed the session that Ry was producing for his album *My Name Is Buddy,* featuring Mike, accordion virtuoso Flaco Jimenez and other amazing players? Listening to a playback in the control room, Mike looked at the computer monitor's display, waveform images from the latest version of Pro Tools dancing along the timeline, and mused, "That's how they do it these days." His mind was back in Appalachia, where he hauled an early reel-to-reel tape recorder along rutted back roads, as he strove to preserve banjo styles that, like exotic plants, thrived in only a few hills and hollers.

And of course, Mike's band mates in the New Lost City Ramblers, Tracy Schwarz and John Cohen, are here. I'm a bit stand-offish with John, who, in a recent unauthorized biography of Doc Watson, has criticized me for keeping Doc from participating in a film score. He doesn't realize that Doc wanted no part of that or any other film gig and that it was my job, as Doc's manager, to play the bad guy, to draw boundaries. (Fortunately, John and I will talk this out and reconcile, a few weeks before his own death, a decade later.)

Pete's ninety-year-old voice is a scratchy shadow of the one that inspired my thirteen-year-old self at that concert in Boston. But he still knows how to lead a song. His longneck banjo is his baton, although sometimes a bony finger helps keep us on track.

After the gathering, we repair to a jam session at Cathy Fink and Marcy Marxer's, where the music flows freely – David Grisman and Tim O'Brien are trading mandolin licks in one corner, Happy Traum and Stefan Grossman comparing guitar instruction techniques in another – as does the wine. And memories of Mike.

From my earliest interest in the music, he is on my radar, although it is a while before I actually meet him and hear his mastery of the full array of mountain music instruments. He is Pete Seeger's half brother, but has chosen a different musical path. Instead of Pete's sense of music as a political tool, Mike is deeply into preserving original styles of what's come to be known as old-time music. Where Pete's group is the Weavers, who sing songs of social protest, Mike is a founding member of the New Lost City Ramblers, who create their repertoire from obscure 78 rpm recordings from the early twentieth century. But both see music as a powerful force to bind communities together.

Early on, the Ramblers create quite a buzz in New York, and word travels to Boston. We hear of a legendary concert in which Mike Seeger ends an encore by smashing a guitar on stage, thereby beating The Who and Jimi Hendrix to the punch by perhaps a decade.

It is The Ballad Room, Manny Greenhill's and George Wein's short-lived experiment in a folk music nightclub, that finally brings the New Lost City Ramblers to Boston, and I attend the first night of their engagement. No guitars are smashed. But, seated just off stage left, I have a terrific view as Mike capos his banjo – regular length neck; no newfangled adaptations for him – and tears into the old murder ballad "Poor Ellen Smith." Seeing him play it, and especially how he uses the capo, unravels some of the recording's mystery, and the music is sublime and haunting. And yet, it is somewhat like hearing a NLCR recording – is that right? Shouldn't there be surprise, new direction?

*What the well-dressed musician wears:*
*The New Lost City Ramblers*

The Copley Hotel's barbershop functions as The Ballad Room's dressing room and backstage area. The first time I meet the band, Mike is sitting in a barber chair, Marge on his lap. They are sweethearts now, soon to be a married couple and parents. The Ramblers have a whole different dress code from either Pete Seeger or Miles Davis: they dress in period suits from the 1930s. When the performance is over, they change into jeans and T-shirts.

Of the band members, Mike is the one who becomes my friend. He stays not only at the family home on Huntoon Street, but also with Louise and me – and later young Matt Greenhill – when we start our family in Cambridge. When we move to California, Mike enlists my band to represent the newer, more electric sounds of the Berkeley music community. And I visit him and Marge at their home in Roosevelt, New Jersey.

*Mike Seeger and dulcimer*

Mike introduces me to the highest level of traditional music: from Cajun masters like Dewey Balfa and Marc Savoy to fingerpicking masters like Elizabeth Cotten, whom he met when his parents, folklorist Charles Seeger and composer Ruth Crawford Seeger, engaged Libba to take care of their children.

In her nineties, Libba Cotten was still performing, including her signature composition "Freight Train," a test that every aspiring fingerpicker had to pass. Her role had changed from young Mike's caretaker to middle-age Mike's headline act. He would open concerts for her, and look after her on the road, a role reversal not lost on either of them.

Mike loves the crucial crossroads where African-American and Appalachian traditions intersect, and this becomes an important lesson for me. As time passes, the African-American side of old-time music occupies an increasingly prominent place in his worldview. He takes up the fretless banjo and the panpipes, reportedly imported from Africa by slaves, and sings the chilling "We Are Stolen Souls From Africa." As his musical interests evolve, he becomes politically closer to Pete and Peggy. By the time he is working with Ry Cooder on *My Name Is Buddy*, he tells me that Ry is bold in forging such a musical critique on the politics of have and have-not. Perhaps it is the specifics of Ry's approach, creating characters rather than preaching abstractions, that appeals to Mike. But the analysis is pretty close to Pete's vision, back when I was thirteen, that we should "own these banks of marble" and "share those vaults of silver that we have sweated for."

Some months after the memorial service, I drive from Washington to Lexington, Virginia. Mike's widow Alexia is working her way through his belongings, including some forty banjos. She has agreed to sell me one.

*Kraske, patent 1902*

At first I'm thinking that a fretless gourd banjo would be cool. But when I try to play one, it soon becomes clear that this instrument is beyond my capabilities. The gourd is hard to hold on my lap, the lack of frets challenges my intonation chops, and the old friction pegs make it a bear to tune. So I explore the remaining stash and find myself drawn to an old Kraske.

There is a printed description: "Hollow wood hoop with bracket tube, similar to Gibson trapdoor, 26-1/2" scale, 26 brackets, patent Dec 9, 1902 on dowel and neck adjustment, dowel stamped V. Kraske Chicago Ill, headstock inlaid with 4 fleur de lis."

And a final message from Mike: "This is one of my especially favorite banjos because of its balance between plunk and clarity and its relative lack of metallic overtones."

Decades removed from when Pete inspired me with union singalongs on the longneck, and from when I subsequently traded the longneck for a Scruggs-style banjo with resonator, I settle into a new relationship with Mike's Kraske. This is more like the banjo that Tom Ashley frailed, back at that early Galax festival. I start to work on Mike's instruction video, "Southern Mountain Banjo Styles." Before too long I can render a passable rendition of "Battle In the Horseshoe."

Still finding my way inside the music.

*Waterbound and I can't get home*
*Waterbound and I can't get home*
*Waterbound and I can't get home*
   *Down to North Carolina*
      *— traditional, as sung by Mike Seeger*

# AFTERWORD

In 1976, I was back in Boston. I had spent fifteen years as a working musician, but it didn't seem to be going anywhere fast. Seemed, in fact, to be in retreat. The folk music boom (or "scare," as we sometimes termed it) was long past, and in retrospect it seemed like a quirky version of the good old days, a time when one could casually work up a few songs on the guitar and play for an interested, perhaps even committed audience. A time when the seeking was as important as the finding. As our scene became more popular, more integral to mainstream culture, it became less precious. Perhaps I knew it was over when I found myself playing from the back of a pickup truck under a sign that read "Hootenanny Used Car Sale." That audience, kicking tires and poking upholstery, was a different creature from the music aficionados at Club 47.

I had found a good and receptive audience in Northern California, during my years with The Frontier. The Frontier toured the west coast, including nearly all the Universities of California, but our home base was the redwood country of Sonoma County. We wrote songs, kept each other company, and eventually drove each other crazy. I learned a lot about country music from Mayne Smith, a lot about songwriting from Mayne, Mark Spoelstra and pianist Dave Holt, and a lot about time from our rhythm section, Michael Woodward and Texas Lee Poundstone, "the Sage of the

Brush." (He had played with Lightnin' Hopkins at the Vulcan Gas Company, back in Houston). And I learned a lot about friendship from our occasional manager Lee Boek, aka Brother Lee Love.

One night I was driving home after rehearsal. My mind was going over the new tune that The Frontier was working out, much as I used to mentally revisit Rolf Cahn's guitar lessons on the subway to Huntoon Street. Only now, instead of the wimpled nuns, workers with lunch pails and book-toting students who would accompany my subway journey, I was navigating a rural road in Sonoma County. Scrub oaks and pine trees stood on either side. In the rear of my Dodge van lay a Fender Twin Reverb amplifier, recently purchased from the band Country Joe and the Fish.

And then, all of a sudden, four or five deer sped across the roadway, directly in front of me – cousins perhaps of the herd that would temporarily adopt me coming home from Marshall, where this tale began. But this time my headlights were on, lighting them up and spooking them. This herd regarded me not as a member, but as a frightening, glaring intruder.

I swerved and avoided one deer, then another. But I couldn't avoid them all. I caught one on her left haunch. She went down and so did my van, which skidded to the roadside, the amp bouncing crazily in the back, and landed awkwardly in a ditch.

I took a moment to gather myself. Shaken, I was able to open the door and check on the deer (dead) and the

*A typical month at the Inn Of the Beginning, Cotati, California*

amp (okay). Not long after, Texas Lee, also on his way home from our rehearsal, drove up and helped me right the vehicle. In the faint moonlight, he took time to make sure that both I and the van were in fit condition, helped me with my cargo, and then went on his way. The sound of his engine grew fainter, and then all was still.

It was a slow and gingerly ride home, but an hour or so later I was hunkered down in my kitchen, under the familiar stand of redwood trees that surrounded the small village where I lived. Nursing a cup of tea and a shot of whiskey, I contemplated a few bruises both to my ribcage and to my sense of safe passage.

Outside, the deer was hanging from her hind legs, her blood trickling down the hill. That winter, as The Frontier prepared to disband, venison was a staple that sustained me.

The band decided to end with a New Year's Eve bash at Uncle Sam's in Sebastopol. As that date drew closer, we played a few last gigs for our home-away-from-home audiences in Sacramento and especially Berkeley, where we booked a Friday-Saturday farewell at the New Orleans House. It was on Saturday morning, recovering from the previous night's exertions, that I suddenly remembered that The Frontier had agreed to perform that afternoon, on the same stage, for a private function – a wedding reception, I think. The night before, my band mates had scattered to various friends' couches and ad-hoc romantic trysts. Now, after coming up empty-handed on a few phone calls, I grew panicky, wondering if the band was going

*Taj Mahal as a student...*

to leave Berkeley badly, blowing off an obligation.

Pondering the alternatives, I spied the tall and unmistakable figure of Taj Mahal walking down Telegraph Avenue. We had maintained sporadic contact since he visited Huntoon Street to pay his respects to Pete Seeger and Sonny Terry. Now he was enjoying the first fruits of his long, successful career. His band with Ry Cooder formed the core of his first Columbia album, and he regularly performed at concerts and dance halls in California and elsewhere.

*... and as a teacher*

Taj was happy to see me, and, amazingly, receptive to helping me through my predicament. The two of us made our way to the New Orleans House, where he took the chair behind Dave Holt's electric piano. And we successfully jammed our way through the wedding reception. The invited guests drank, danced and schmoozed, and The Frontier's reputation survived intact. That evening, when the guys showed up for the regular gig, there was general regret, both at the lapsed booking and at missing Taj Mahal.

Some years later, I became Taj's agent. "I run into you at the strangest times," he recalled. "Keeps me on my toes."

My daughter Tej was an infant during this period. She often slept in a dressing room, under my scratchy wool poncho. One day I strapped her into a car seat next to me and drove up the coast, towards Mendocino. We were a bit farther north than where I first saw the Pacific Ocean and where I briefly joined a herd of deer, but my taste for the north coast's wild natural splendor remained strong. A couple of California grey whales swam parallel to Route 1, alongside us. "Look!" I cried to Tej, eager to share this special moment. But the one-year-old continued to be fascinated with her own toes, to which she gurgled admiringly.

Matt, just starting grade school, sometimes came on the band's road trips. He would sit on the bus driver's lap while sporting a pair of sunglasses several sizes too big, all cool attitude. "Daddy," he asked shyly one day, as I was packing for a gig, "Can I carry your wa-wa pedal?" Now, in my dotage, I could use the help.

As 1972 turned into 1973, and The Frontier disbanded, I found work as guitarist in a series of local country-western bands, including with Ace Adkins and his Country Boys at the Trail Inn in Santa Rosa. We usually played four sets per night, four nights per week, with an extra couple of sets for the matinee on Sunday. Santa Rosa's country-western radio station broadcast the matinee live. Ace would generally raffle a watermelon as a door prize, a perk from his day job driving an RC Cola delivery truck to the markets around Sonoma County.

As a Country Boy, I welcomed the reduced responsibilities. I now had to merely show up and play, while Ace worried about bookings and relationships with the club owners. And it was fun to learn the guitar styles of a new set of masters, like Roy Nichols, James Burton and Don Rich, who anchored bands led by Merle Haggard and Buck Owens. It was another step into the world of country music that began when I knocked on Merle Travis' hotel room door and would continue in Nashville recording studios with Doc and Merle Watson. But the rowdy atmosphere of the clubs began to wear thin, especially when motorcycle gangs began to find them good places to go and fight.

In my brief return to Boston, I sought out rhythm-and-blues bands, and played regularly in Roxbury, not far from where I first heard Sister Rosetta Tharpe. That worked okay until disco became popular. I remember showing up for a gig at a Masonic Lodge, only to find that our leader had replaced the band with a sound system, and was spinning records instead of singing. I retreated to my van with Calvin the organist, his heavy Hammond B3 lying prone behind us, like an extinct fossil.

Calvin and I played a few gigs as a duo, including a fashion show or two, but the writing was on the wall. By the time my father called with some important news, I was playing top 40 hits at Louie's Lounge in Boston, five sets a night. One night the bass player slipped me a Percocet, and the time passed more quickly. Some of the songs resonated with me, but many did not. In either case, it seemed a long way from what drew me to a musical life, the interaction – almost a dialectic – between deep tradition and creative originality.

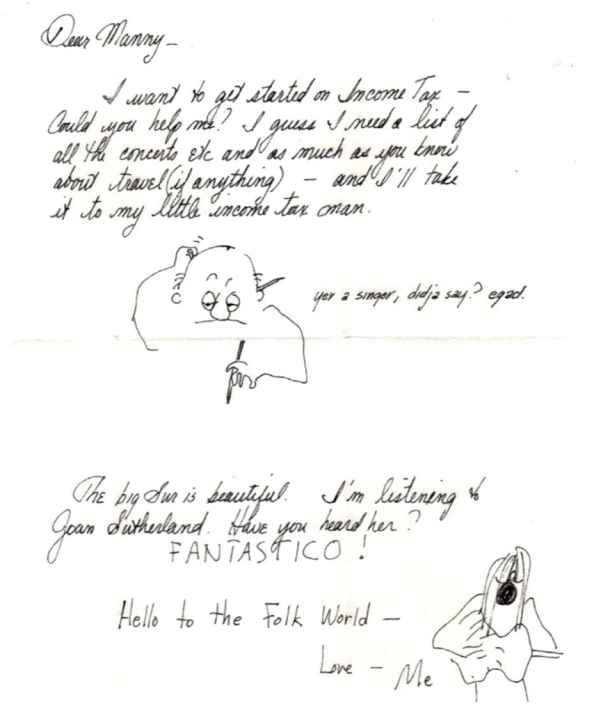

> Dear Manny –
>
> I want to get started on Income Tax – Could you help me? I guess I need a list of all the concerts etc and as much as you know about travel (if anything) – and I'll take it to my little income tax man.
>
> *yer a singer, did ja say? egad.*
>
> The big Sun is beautiful. I'm listening to Joan Sutherland. Have you heard her? FANTASTICO!
>
> Hello to the Folk World –
>
> Love – Me

*Joan and Manny discuss business.*

Dear Joan Baez,

I remember first hearing you sing at Club 47, alternating nights with Eric von Schmidt's blues and Sam Rivers's jazz. I was enthralled at first, but then developed some critical distance. At the time, I told myself it was because you weren't funky enough. But I think my motivations were more complicated.

This folk music has turned out to be more complex than I thought. What is it, anyway? The ballads and protest songs that you wrap your special voice around? The blues that I've been chasing? Or is it music sung not on a stage, but in daily life, washing dishes or mining coal? Sometimes I feel that we humans are mere vessels, transporting the songs from one generation to the next.

When this music came into my life, things changed, especially when my dad started managing you. He used to say that it started at a political rally, where Al Baez, your dad, was speaking as a scientist concerned about nuclear bombs. When Al introduced you to sing a few songs, Manny's ears perked up. When he moved on to a teaching gig in a different town, Al asked Manny to look after you, his teenage daughter, and Folklore suddenly had a new mission, artist representation. That drew my dad's attention to you, and away from me. I didn't see him as much. In his place was this mysterious music, which connected me to him, even as it pulled us apart.
Now, as you're moving on, I'm moving in. I'm sitting at a desk with a telephone. And my father is in the next room, ready to guide me on a new path.

My "Dear Joan" letter

*Joan and Manny, early on*  *Joan and Mitch, later on*

I was beginning to question my commitment to performing music. If this was a calling, the voice was sounding weaker, thinner, and further from the stages where I was playing.

My father's news was that Joan Baez, his original management client, was leaving the company. He was shaken, perhaps wondering if his business, now based in Southern California, would survive.

For me, it was yet another occasion – and Folklore Productions seemed to provide them on a regular basis – to ponder divided loyalties. Did my allegiance lie in my pursuit of an artistic vision, my own aesthetic journey? Or would family ties – not only to my father but also to my children, whose regular needs now included dental checkups and the like – prevail? To this thirty-two year old, it seemed a life choice of big consequence.

Putting aside my purist objections to the business side of music, I offered to join my dad and Folklore Productions. It's an open question as to who was offering a favor to whom; but each of us accepted.

And that's where I've been ever since. I began my career at the company by transcribing lead sheets, including Doc Watson's guitar solos. This was useful and educational, but I soon found that booking gigs was more useful and where the power lay. The first tour that I booked was for Tom Paley. Tom had been a founding member of the New Lost City Ramblers, whom I had met back in The Ballad Room.

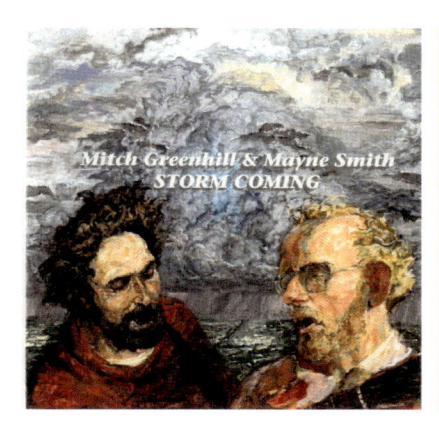

Since leaving the Ramblers, Tom had been living in Britain, and he had somewhat fallen out of the American musical conversation. So booking the tour was a challenge. I struggled with putting together a string of gigs that made both financial and geographical sense. When it was over and all the gigs had played, I felt like I had not succeeded. But when Manny said that I had done a good job, I cheered up a bit and was ready to try again.

Things got a bit easier when Dave Van Ronk asked us to represent him. And once I was trusted to book Doc Watson's concerts

– and later those of Taj Mahal, the Klezmatics, and a host of others – people would return my calls and value what I had to say. It took me a while to see things from presenters' perspectives; but the performers' perspectives were hard-wired into me from the get-go.

I didn't abandon my musical chops. Mayne Smith and I released three albums as a duo, and my current band String Madness has released a second album. I produced recordings for the likes of John Renbourn, Dave Van Ronk, Rosalie Sorrels, and Doc & Merle Watson – one of those, Doc & Merle's "Big Sandy/Leather Britches," won a Grammy. After meeting theater director Roberta Levitow, whom I was fortunate enough to marry in 1995, I composed music and designed sound for regional theaters – one of those, *An Almost Holy Picture*, made its way to Broadway.

Instead of continuing to play full time, I became more devoted to furthering the careers of other, better musicians, artists truly plugged in to music as a life force, who were deeper inside the music than I would ever reach. They became my focus. In some cases, the artists' generational relay race, handing the baton from father to son, has mirrored that of the Greenhill clan. I remember, for example, hearing Leon Bibb sing at the Ballad Room, back in my early teens; now we represent his son Eric. And my relationship with Marc and Ann Savoy, who introduced me to Cajun culture back at Mardi Gras 1983, now extends to their son Wilson, leader of the Pine Leaf Boys, who was one year old at the time.

Manny Greenhill, like so many others in these pages, passed away, felled by leukemia in 1996. His was a full and interesting life, one that began in an insular enclave of Eastern European Jews who migrated to New York in the late nineteenth or early twentieth century. This community generally viewed the world as divided between abused Jews and abusive Christians. Politics, particularly opposition to the rise of fascism in the 1930's, offered Manny a way out, a bridge to a broader vision of humanity.

*Manny, Mitch at Folklore Productions office, Santa Monica*

He came to see a different dichotomy, the divide between rich and poor, between haves and have-nots, or, as he generally saw it, between management and labor. Music was more than a background to this political awakening; it was a social tool, a way to spread the vision to others. That's what made Pete Seeger and Joan Baez so important to him, the way their music resonated beyond the concert hall to bigger concerns. The People's Music, he called it. "Pete Seeger is the Johnny Appleseed of folk music," he would say, "and I am one of his seedlings."

Now that he is gone, I finally grasp my father's life in full: The young Mendel, formally photographed in long curls and short pants, who rebelled against his own father, a stern and severe man who spent the Sabbath in pursuit of his passion as cantor to a storefront synagogue, while toiling away during the week as a fabric-cutter in the *schmatte* trade. Manny the college student, now sporting a beard and playing guitar, jolted by the Spanish Civil War into a political awakening that never faded. The labor activist who managed to serve in World War II, despite two rejections because of a collapsed lung. Failed attempts at careers as a watch repairman and venetian blind salesman. Founder of a small business soliciting advertisements for ethnic newspapers. (One of my first jobs was calling local businesses to ask if they would kindly renew their ads in the annual Pulaski Day edition of *The Polish Daily Courier*.) And finally, impresario, artist manager, *bon vivant*, world traveler, and general *mensch*.

Throughout his life, he remained open to the unexpected, and retained the ability to be surprised. I remember him, a few months before his death, as we attended a meeting of the Folk Alliance, an organization that would posthumously honor him with a Lifetime Achievement Award. Manny was standing in the hotel lobby, listening intently to a pretty good look-at-your-shoes bluegrass band. His expression was one of charmed delight, as if he expected, at any moment, to hear something new and revelatory.

After public memorials in Santa Monica and Cambridge, Harold Leventhal convened a private gathering in New York. As manager to the likes of Pete Seeger, Arlo Guthrie and Judy Collins, Harold had known Manny well. And, over the years, he became a sort of surrogate uncle to me, as well. When in New York, I got in the habit of dropping by his midtown office to soak up stories of his wartime stint in India, his apprenticeship as song-plugger for Irving Berlin, and his gradual disenchantment with the Communist Party. "How did you quit the party?" I once asked. "One year I just stopped paying dues," was his down-to-earth reply.

The politics that dare not speak its name was a history shared by a number of the older attendees at this memorial gathering. After a few drinks had somewhat loosened the conversation, someone asked Harold where he had met Pete Seeger. "We were in the same Communist cell," he replied. Steve Gardner, who had re-

*Harold Leventhal*

cently suffered a heart attack and was just beginning to venture outside his own apartment, summoned his strength to rise to his feet and thunder, "You *never* say that! You say *'Me and a certain other person* were in the same Communist cell!'" Then, exhausted, Steve sank back into the plush couch.

I looked around at Harold's spacious pre-war apartment, just across from Riverside Park and Pete's beloved Hudson River. Harold's wife and my mother were uncomfortably gazing at the ceiling. Before I could stop myself, I asked how, as a strong critic of capitalist economics, he nonetheless managed to achieve considerable financial success within it. "Well," Harold summarized, unfazed, "we on the left were always good organizers." And then poured another round of drinks.

The company that Manny Greenhill founded continues. My son Matt joined shortly after his grandfather's death. He carries himself with a social grace and ease that reminds me of the old man. We make a good team.

Now in my 70s, part of me wants to step back a bit, spend more time with Roberta, visit with my children, mentor my grandchildren. Another part of me wants to learn more about the guitar, more about the music that has inspired me. And yet another part wants to hear new music and visit new places. I'm hearing great things about the scene in Cartagena, Colombia, and I've never been to South America.

In 2004 I spent my sixtieth birthday walking the streets of Focşani, Romania, the town where my maternal grandmother was raised. She had always talked about a big river that ran through the center of town, a crucial childhood setting. If jazz reached middle America by steaming up the mighty Mississippi from New Orleans, our family's creation myth sprang from the river that ran through Focşani, where Grandma Minnie played as a girl. I stood in the center of town and looked for it in every direction, but it was nowhere to be found. So I asked about it and was told, by those old enough to remember, that it had been just a trickle of a creek, long since paved over.

I wonder if my memory of Paul Robeson is like that. Maybe it was a small concert in a modest room, one that Robeson quickly forgot. But to me, a wellspring that still nurtures.

*In Romania, 2004*

# ACKNOWLEDGEMENTS

I am most indebted to my wife Roberta Levitow, who first encouraged me to write, then read early drafts, and gave wise counsel throughout the process.

Allan Evans, James Field, Larry Mollin, Kit Rachlis, Wade Schuman and Mayne Smith read the work in progress and gave informed and helpful insights. So did Mary Katherine Aldin, who also served as proofreader. Monona Wali gave valuable instruction during my semester at Santa Monica College. Wyn Cooper edited the manuscript. They helped make the text better.

The Book Designers—Alan Dino Hebel and Ian Koviak — designed the book. Susan Dworski gave valuable input on cover design.

Thanks to generous photographers including Dick Waterman, Chris Strachwitz, Stefan Grossman, Bruce Jackson, Jon Hancock and the estate of John Byrne Cooke. Wolfgang Frank of Concord Music Group kindly gave permission to use archival photos, including album covers.

Everything described in these pages did happen. But I have used my imagination in recreating dialogue, and have at times conflated and compressed events and characters. In particular, "Uncle" Steve Gardner is a combination of several avuncular guides to my coming of age, including Margie and Jimmy McCluskey and Estelle Epstein.

Estelle especially was one of a kind. She and my mother met in kindergarten and maintained a close friendship until the end of their days – through college, career, family, and the politics that dare not speak its name.

Like Steve, Estelle took me under her wing and made sure that I was exposed to some of life's finer things, like Duke Ellington, the newly-opened Guggenheim Museum, and the picket line.

It's hard to accept that I will no longer hear the clanking of Estelle's political buttons denouncing, in capital letters, the latest corporate rape of Brooklyn, the government's current colonialist military adventure, and her final enemies: mayors Rudy Giuliani and Michael Bloomberg.

If there is an afterlife, I am sure that Estelle has cornered some unsuspecting member of the service economy there, some angel or cherub, and is leaning over, whispering confidentially, "So, tell me – how are the working conditions?"

She, like so many others I encountered, faced life with a fierce passion. If more of us followed their examples, the world would, I feel, be a better place.

As I remember, I'll toast my mentors and play an album. This time, let's make it

*Estelle Epstein vs. the ruling class*

a long-playing vinyl record, rather than one of its newfangled digital successors. My younger, questioning self moved in tempo with these albums, at 33 and 1/3 revolutions per minute.

The needle softly lands and the music begins to play. The outer grooves, where the music establishes itself, take longer to revolve. I think of my formative years, the ones recalled in these pages, like that – full, rich, almost overflowing (or distorting?) with experience. Here in the inner grooves of my later life, closer to the abyss of the central spindle hole, the cycles follow more quickly, one after the other.

    The music plays on.

# PHOTO CREDITS

Foreword: Running with the Herd
    Run Doe Run – oil painting by Tej Greenhill
    Mitch with beard and Telecaster – photographer unknown

5 Years Old: I Hear a Song
    Paul Robeson – courtesy of Vanguard Records/Craft Recordings A division of Concord
    First guitar lesson – Greenhill family archive
    Sister Rosetta Tharpe – publicity shot
    W.C. Handy – publicity shot

13 Years Old: Ice Skating with Pete Seeger
    Weavers at Carnegie Hall album cover – courtesy Concord Music Group
    Advertising Pete Seeger – Folklore Inc. archive
    FBI file on Manny – Folklore Inc. archive, photo by Mitch
    Informal ice rink – photographer unknown
    Manny, Pete backstage – Folklore Inc. archive, photo by Julie Snow
    Seeger family – courtesy Seeger family archive
    Pete, Matt, Mitch, Klezmatics at Clearwater Festival – photo by Roberta Levitow

A Surrogate Uncle, and What the Well-Dressed Musician Will Wear
    Steve Gardner – courtesy the Gardner family
    Miles Davis – publicity shot
    Pete Seeger – photo by Bruce Jackson
    Miles Davis – publicity shot

14 Years Old: Theory and Practice with Rolf Cahn
    Rolf Cahn – photographer unknown
    Rolf letter to Manny – Folklore Inc. archive
    Debbie Green and Rolf – photographer unknown
    Rolf Cahn – photographer unknown
    Rolf and contraband – photo by Mitch

4 Huntoon Street, Dorchester Lower Mills: A Parade of Musical Visitors
    Sonny Terry & Brownie McGhee – photo by Dick Waterman
    Sonny Terry – photo by Dick Waterman
    Ballad Room advertisement – Folklore Inc. archive
    Manny and Bob Dylan – Folklore Inc. archive
    4 Huntoon Street then – Greenhill family archive
    Odetta's E7 chord – photo by Mitch
    4 Huntoon Street now – photo by Roberta Levitow
    Manny and Leona 1943 – Greenhill family archive

14 Years Old: Saturday Night and Sunday Morning with Reverend Gary Davis
    Reverend Davis with Miss Gibson – photo by Dick Waterman
    Reverend Davis's C7 chord – photo by Mitch
    Reverend and Annie Davis – photo by Dick Waterman
    Reverend Davis with 12-string and cigar – publicity photo courtesy Stefan Grossman
    Reverend Davis in repose – photo by Dick Waterman

15 Years Old: The Artist's Life with Eric von Schmidt
    Mitch, Rolf, Eric – Folklore Inc. archive
    Eric, Mitch, Maria at Newport Folk Festival – Folklore Inc. archive
    New Years Greeting – by Eric von Schmidt
    Eric accompanied by Mitch – photo by Dick Waterman
    Eric, Muldaurs, Mitch at Newport – photographer unknown
    Caitlin von Schmidt and Papa – photo by Mary Eastman

15 Years Old: Divided Loyalties with Merle Travis
    Merle Travis – publicity shot
    Merle Travis in Boston 1959 album cover – courtesy Concord Music Group

16 Years Old: Breaking Boundaries with Lightnin' Hopkins
    Lightnin' Hopkins – publicity photo courtesy Stefan Grossman
    Lightnin' Hopkins – publicity photo courtesy Stefan Grossman
    Lightnin', Mitch, Chris Strachwitz at Newport Folk Festival – photo by Dick Waterman
    Mitch, Lightnin', Louise at Newport Folk Festival – photo by Manny Greenhill
    Lightnin' Hopkins – publicity photo courtesy Stefan Grossman
    Lightnin' in Houston – photo by Chris Strachwitz © Arhoolie Foundation

16-20 Years Old: A Wider World with Jackie Washington
    Advertisement – Folklore Inc. archive
    Accompanying Jack — Folklore Inc. archive
    Mitch, Louise, Mississippi John Hurt, Jerry Ricks — Folklore Inc. archive

Fritz, Mitch accompany Jack – Folklore Inc. archive
Leona, Eric, Jack – Greenhill/Folklore archive
Leona Greenhill – photo by Mitch
Pete sends regrets – Greenhill/Folklore archive

The Big City: New York
    Barbecue Bob – publicity shot
    Barbecue Bob – publicity shot
    Dave Van Ronk album cover – courtesy Concord Music Group
    Jesse Fuller album cover – courtesy Concord Music Group
    Jesse Fuller – photo by Dick Waterman
    Jesse Fuller at CBC – Folklore Inc. archive

The Big Country: Inside of the Outside
    Tom Ashley – photo by Bob Yellin
    Chez Savoy – photographer unknown

The Big World: Larger Struggles
    Freedom Singers – © John Byrne Cooke LLC

17-22 Years Old: Geoff Muldaur's School of Hip, and the Cambridge-Boston Music Scene
    Bob Gibson, Joan Baez at Newport Folk Festival – photo by Lawrence Shustak, courtesy Joan Baez, Meridian Green
    Geoff Muldaur – photo by Dick Waterman
    Mitch, Geoff at Newport Folk Festival – Greenhill family archive, photographer unknown
    Von Schmidts, Greenhill, Muldaurs at Newport Folk Festival – Greenhill family archive, photographer unknown
    Skip James at Newport Folk Festival – photo by Dick Waterman

Fahey self-portrait – © John Fahey Trust
Jim Kweskin Jug Band at Newport Folk Festival – © John Byrne Cooke LLC
Mitch, Jeff Gutcheon – Greenhill/Folklore archive
Mitch accompany Rosalie Sorrels – photographer unknown
Revisiting Aquinnah – photo by Roberta Levitow
Moshup's creation – photo by Roberta Levitow

20 Years Old: Recording with Sam Charters
Sam Charters, Danny Kalb, Dave Van Ronk – courtesy Andrea Vuocolo, Dave Van Ronk estate
Charters letter to Manny – Folklore Inc. archive
Dave Van Ronk, Sam Charters Ronk – courtesy Andrea Vuocolo, Dave Van Ronk estate
*Shepherd of the Highways* album cover by Eric von Schmidt, courtesy Concord Music Group

Wanderlust: Target Practice with Hunter Thompson
Rosalie Sorrels album cover
Joseph Spence – photo by Dick Waterman
Spence letter to Mitch – Greenhill family archive

23 Years Old: On to California
The Frontier at Uncle Sam's – publicity photo

The View from Doc Watson's Funeral
Bozo twelve-string guitar – photo by Mitch
Doc and Mitch at Merlefest – photo by Jon Hancock

The View from Mike Seeger's Memorial
New Lost City Ramblers – publicity shot
Mike Seeger and dulcimer – photo by Bruce Jackson
Kraske banjo – photo by Mitch

Afterword
> Taj as student – photo by Dick Waterman
> Taj as teacher – photo by Dick Waterman
> Joan letter to Manny – Folklore Inc. archive
> Joan and Manny – Folklore Inc. archive
> Joan and Mitch – photographer unknown
> Album covers: *Storm Coming* by Eric von Schmidt. *Live 1976* by Roberta Levitow. *String Madness* by Roberta Levitow & String Madness. *Eye of the Beholder* by Roberta Levitow.
> Manny and Mitch – Folklore Inc. archive
> Harold Leventhal – photo by Mitch
> Mitch in Romania – photo by Mitch

Acknowledgements
> Estelle Epstein – photographer unknown

Front cover
> Gibson L1 – photo by Mitch

Rear cover
> Mitch Greenhill – photo by Roberta Levitow
> Reverend Gary Davis – photo by Dick Waterman
> Lightnin' Hopkins – photo by Chris Strachwitz © Arhoolie Foundation
> Doc Watson and Mitch Greenhill – photo by Jon Hancock
> Pete Seeger advertisement – Folklore Inc. archive
> Other photographers unknown

PLAYLIST AVAILABLE AT
*www.youtube.com
/playlist?list=PLO_k09aU7uwvKs6Z6mfMDZmY0UQjvUooD*

Made in the USA
San Bernardino, CA
20 April 2020